SALT AND LIGHT

SALT AND LIGHT

THE COMMANDMENTS, THE BEATITUDES, *and a* JOYFUL LIFE

MARK P. SHEA

PUBLISHED BY FRANCISCAN MEDIA
Cincinnati, Ohio

Cover and book design by Mark Sullivan
Cover image © Fotolia | Marilyn Barbone

LIBRARY OF CONGRESS CATALOGING-IN-PUBLICATION DATA
Shea, Mark P.
Salt and light : the Commandments, the Beatitudes, and a joyful life / Mark P. Shea.
     p. cm.
Includes bibliographical references.
ISBN 978-1-61636-496-0 (alk. paper)
1. Ten commandments. 2. Beatitudes. 3. Catholic Church—Doctrines. I. Title.
BV4655.S495 2013
241.5'2—dc23
                    2012036683

Published by Servant Books, an imprint of Franciscan Media
28 W. Liberty St.
Cincinnati, OH 45202
www.FranciscanMedia.org

Printed in the United States of America.
Printed on acid-free paper.
13 14 15 16 17 5 4 3 2 1

To Janet, Luke, Tasha, Lucy, Cow,
Claire, Peter, and Sean,
whom I love with all my heart.

And to Blessed Sacrament Parish,
my microcosm of the Wedding Feast.

CONTENTS

Acknowledgments, *ix*
Introduction, *xi*

PART ONE: THE TEN COMMANDMENTS, *1*
Chapter 1:   The First Commandment: *No Other Gods, 5*
Chapter 1.5:   The 1.5 Commandment: *Concerning Images, 14*
Chapter 2:   The Second Commandment: *Hallow God's Name, 19*
Chapter 3:   The Third Commandment: *Honor the Sabbath, 26*
Chapter 4:   The Fourth Commandment: *Honor Your Father and Mother, 31*
Chapter 5:   The Fifth Commandment: *Against Murder, 39*
Chapter 6:   The Sixth Commandment: *Against Adultery, 55*
Chapter 7:   The Seventh Commandment: *Against Theft, 61*
Chapter 8:   The Eighth Commandment: *Against Bearing False Witness, 67*
Chapter 9:   The Ninth Commandment: *Against Coveting Your Neighbor's Spouse, 85*
Chapter 10:   The Tenth Commandment: *Against Coveting Your Neighbor's Goods, 92*

PART TWO: THE BEATITUDES, *95*
Chapter 11:   *Blessed Are the Poor in Spirit, 97*
Chapter 12:   *Blessed Are Those Who Mourn, 100*
Chapter 13:   *Blessed Are the Meek, 105*
Chapter 14:   *Blessed Are Those Who Hunger and Thirst for Righteousness, 109*
Chapter 15:   *Blessed Are the Merciful, 115*
Chapter 16:   *Blessed Are the Pure in Heart, 120*

Chapter 17:   *Blessed Are the Peacemakers, 130*
Chapter 18:   *Blessed Are Those Persecuted for Righteousness'*
              Sake, 138
Chapter 19:   *Blessed Are Those Persecuted for Christ, 143*

Bibliography, *153*
Notes, *154*

ACKNOWLEDGMENTS

Thanks above all to God, the Father, Son, and Holy Spirit, from whom, to whom, and through whom this book and all things exist. Blessed be he!

Thanks also to
- the good people at Franciscan Media;
- the good folk who read my blog *Catholic and Enjoying It!*
- Dave and Sherry Curp and all the Curplings;
- my dear friend Sherry Weddell and the gang at the Catherine of Siena Institute in Colorado Springs, Colorado (You guys do awesome work!);
- Dale Ahlquist, president of the G.K. Chesterton Society, for being such a thoughtful and funny guy—like Chesterton, only thinner.

And special thanks to Sts. Jerome, Athanasius, Anthony of the Desert, Francis de Sales, Dominic, Tertius, and of course, Mama Mary, on whose constant intercession I rely for help. *Ora pro nobis.*

There is a famous *Far Side* cartoon that describes what we say to our dogs ("Did you get into the trash, Ginger? You've been a bad dog! Don't do that, Ginger!") versus what our dogs hear ("Blah blah blah, GINGER, blah blah blah, GINGER!"). If all you had to go on was what you see in the media, you'd get the impression that when the Church speaks, what our watchdogs in the press hear is "Blah blah blah, SEX, blah blah blah, SEX." Catholic moral teaching, in the world's eyes, more or less begins and ends with sex.

For instance, Pope Benedict XVI writes an entire encyclical called *God Is Love*, in which he reflects on the profundities of God's revelation in Christ, and *The New York Times* can only think to say, with some mystification, that it does "not mention abortion, homosexuality, contraception or divorce, issues that often divide Catholics."[1]

Such observations are then punctuated with the eye-roll-inducing complaint that the Church is obsessed with sex and talks of nothing else.

In short, our manufacturers of secular culture overlook vast oceans of Catholic moral reflection that have given us everything from the hospital to the university to the most immense network of charitable works on the planet. That's bad because even most Catholics get what information they have about their own faith not from the Church, but from that media via chat around the water cooler, or something they dimly remember reading on the Internet, or stuff on TV. The average person, including the average Catholic, "knows" what he "knows" about Catholic teaching mainly from a pop culture media that is fundamentally clueless about the Church, plus whatever strange additions or subtractions may enter the mix from our own muddled heads or the heads of our acquaintances. That leads directly to a sort of feedback loop that shows up, not only in the media, but everywhere in contemporary culture that makes us more and more fuddled about the things that our loving God desires we understand with more and more clarity.

I well remember, for instance, the sweet, concerned friend who worried about the crisis of faith I must have been facing when Pope John Paul II was badly injured in a fall in the early nineties. When I responded with surprise and confusion over her grave concern for the stability of my faith, she said, "Well, I know Catholics believe the pope is *indestructible* and all..." Still other times I have encountered (former) Catholics who confidently inform me that the Trinity "went out with Vatican II." And the number of people—including Catholics—who took seriously the absurd claims of *The Da Vinci Code* in preference to the accounts of Jesus in the New Testament bears eloquent witness to the baleful effects of learning our faith from giant media conglomerates instead of from eyewitnesses to the Resurrection who paid for their faith in Jesus with their own blood.

It therefore is advisable—for those who wish to find out more about the Catholic moral tradition than the media allows us to know—to take a look at the roots of that tradition as it has been proposed to us by the Church for two thousand years. The place to do that is the *Catechism of the Catholic Church*, which shows us the actual roots of the Catholic moral tradition. And that means taking a look at two basic sources: the Ten Commandments and the Beatitudes.

The Ten Commandments are the indispensable foundation for the Christian understanding of the moral life. A house without a foundation is a house doomed to collapse. And in this world populated by fallen human beings, collapse is generally imminent. So the Law is crucial because it is the thing that keeps us, who are prone to doing evil, in check. It is also the thing that, as we shall see, provides the best tool for pinpointing the sin in our souls that is the cause of the collapse.

Some people suppose the Ten Commandments are pretty much all you need for Catholic moral teaching. Hew to the Law and you'll be a moral person, it is thought. And being a moral person is what Christianity is all about, right?

Actually, wrong. Morality is a good thing, to be sure, but the Catholic faith does not call us to be merely moral any more than good spelling is all that is required for a Ph.D. in English literature. Sainthood—which is, after all, the primary thing the Catholic faith exists to help us achieve—demands something much greater: "For I tell you, unless your righteousness exceeds that of the scribes and Pharisees, you will never enter the kingdom of heaven" (Matthew 5:20).

Of course, we are given that righteousness by grace through faith in Jesus Christ, since nobody can be justified before God merely by clenching his teeth and trying to obey the Law. But the fact that we are justified by grace through faith does not mean "Meet the minimum requirements—no blaspheming, killing, or cheating on your wife—and you are saved." One man famously thought this was the program and received a startling correction:

> And a ruler asked him, "Good Teacher, what shall I do to inherit eternal life?" And Jesus said to him, "Why do you call me good? No one is good but God alone. You know the commandments: 'Do not commit adultery, Do not kill, Do not steal, Do not bear false witness, Honor your father and mother.'" And he said, "All these I have observed from my youth." And when Jesus heard it, he said to him, "One thing you still lack. Sell all that you have and distribute to the poor, and you will have treasure in heaven; and come, follow me." But when he heard this he became sad, for he was very rich. (Luke 18:18–23)

In other words, in Christ the commandments form the bottom, not the top, of the Christian moral life. You can't go below them, but you can reach far above them. The idea behind the commandments is, "If you can't love God, at least don't blaspheme him by worshiping false gods. If you can't love your neighbor, at least don't rob him, canoodle his wife, or beat him to death with a baseball bat." We're not exactly looking at the snow-capped summits of human moral endeavor here. We are instead looking at the lowest expectations that can be placed on the human person for minimum decency—and even those are more than many people can muster.

"Many people" includes many of us Christians. We can be inveterate jailhouse lawyers when it comes to God's demands for sanctity. We often hold out for Minimum Daily Adult Requirement Christianity, asking how little we have to obey God and how much selfishness we can get away with and still be saved. This approach to discipleship is something like a bride who asks on her wedding night, "How many times do I have to kiss my husband in order to fulfill the Church's definition of a 'good wife'?"

There's a fundamental tone deafness at work whenever we greet the love of God with plea bargaining and attempts to minimize his demands for obedience. God's grace is not given to us with the exhortation, "See that you get as close to mortal sin as you can without technically committing it." Rather, it is given in order to make us saints.

Jesus gave us the Beatitudes to teach us that the goal is to actually *love* God and neighbor with all our heart, soul, mind, and strength, not merely get away with venial sin and minimal obedience. They remind us that the purpose of the Christian life is not ice-cold rule keeping but *happiness*—total, unending, ecstatic, fiery joy. This joy is far closer to the ecstasy of great sex with the love of your life than it is to getting one's sums right in a math quiz. In short, the Beatitudes point us not to the bottom of the moral ladder but to the top, which reaches into heaven itself.

If you think I'm being irreverent in comparing heaven to the marital act, reflect on the fact that marriage is a sacrament and that both the Old and New Testaments constantly compare our relationship with God to that of man and wife (see the book of Hosea, for example, as well as Isaiah 54:5 and Ephesians 5:21–32). Of course, God is vastly more *unlike* than like anything he has made, including the creation called marriage. But nonetheless he did not choose marriage at random to reflect and communicate some of his glory. Jesus, whose first miracle was done at a wedding, constantly compares the kingdom of heaven to a wedding banquet, and the book of Revelation reaches its climax in the marriage supper of the Lamb (see John 2:1–11; Matthew 22:1–14; Revelation 19—21).

Of course, when the world thinks of heaven, it thinks of beautiful scenery, of various perks like immortal youth and health, or of a vague luminosity. And to be sure, heaven will be the most beautiful place imaginable (and it will involve the *place* called the new earth—see Revelation 21:1—not simply vaporous spooks floating in the vast nowhere). But that's not what captures the biblical imagination. Rather, the supreme joy of heaven is that we shall see God "face to face" (1 Corinthians 13:12). That is the essence of beatitude. So Jesus, in the Beatitudes, trains our eyes, so to speak, to see the face of God in the poor, the mourning, the meek, the persecuted, and all the others whom he names "blessed." Indeed, he is training us not merely to see those faces but to wear them.

That strikes a lot of people as a downer. We'd much rather see God's face in some cool mystical trance without all the fuss and bother of those tacky people and their intrusive problems that mess up our day. As a general rule we'd also rather not have to look ourselves squarely in the eye. But the Ten Commandments and the Beatitudes are firm on the matter: If we want to see God's face, we must confront the twin fact that we are sinners and that we have the awe-inspiring chance to become saints.

Looking at God's face requires us to look at our own face and that of our neighbor with unblinking and courageous eyes. We have to "face" the fact that we all wear masks of sin that must be removed (which is why we need the Law—to alert us to our sins). And we have to embrace the fact that Christ is here not to condemn but to save us and to bring us to eternal ecstasy and, well, beatitude.

Indeed Christ is quite open about his promise to give us what we most deeply want—what we cannot, in fact, *not* want: happiness. He has no truck with any moral theory that tells us we should not desire happiness. In fact, the Faith explicitly denies that it is even *possible* for us to not desire happiness. The only thing we can do is desire and attempt to gain happiness in right or wrong ways.

Every act of virtue has as its ultimate goal the ordered pursuit of happiness. Every sin is a disordered love of some good—in short, a grab at happiness done wrongly. It's not wrong to seek sexual pleasure, but it is wrong to steal another person's spouse to obtain it. It's not wrong to enjoy the taste of food, but it is wrong to eat more than is healthy for us. It's not wrong to have money, but it is wrong to beat up a third-grader and take the five bucks his mom put in his pocket for his lunch. Because of our tendency to look for happiness in all the wrong ways, Jesus gives us the Beatitudes: a series of highly counterintuitive prescriptions for finding happiness in such unlikely places as soup kitchens, graveyards, and gallows. Without them we will act by the light of our fallen intellect, weakened will, and disordered appetites. These tell us that it is crazy to lose our life in order to save it and that the war of all against all is the iron law of existence.

The Church, in contrast, says that since we are going to seek happiness no matter what—and since the perpetual attempts to get it from money, sex, and power never work—we should do it by following the directions given by him who is Happiness. For of course the only reason for trusting that the Beatitudes aren't crazy is that Jesus teaches them and has lived them with happy results himself, followed by a long train of jittery disciples who, nerved to do so by the Resurrection, gave them a try and found out that, crazy as they sound, they really do lead to happiness. The testimony of the Catholic Tradition is that if you are nervous about this whole "losing your life to find it" thing (and who isn't?), you should listen to the voices of our ancestors in the faith who have field-tested the Beatitudes in the crucible of experience and reported a massive amount of customer satisfaction, much to their surprise.

> Therefore, since we are surrounded by so great a cloud of witnesses, let us also lay aside every weight, and sin which clings so closely, and let us run with perseverance the race that is set before us, looking to Jesus the pioneer and perfecter of our faith, who for the joy that was set before him endured the cross, despising the shame, and is seated at the right hand of the throne of God.
>
> Consider him who endured from sinners such hostility against himself, so that you may not grow weary or fainthearted (Hebrews 12:1–3).

So in this journey into the moral life of the Church, we will look at these twin pillars of the Catholic moral life—the Ten Commandments and the Beatitudes—as the means of training our eyes to look for the kingdom of heaven. If we were already virtuous there would be no need for the Law. But since we are fallen, the Law helps us deal with the fact of our brokenness, both punishing evil and leading us toward the Savior. And the Savior gives us the power to find our ultimate happiness—our beatitude—in his teaching and in the gift of the Holy Spirit, who helps us live it out. Let's take a walk down that road.

PART ONE

The Ten Commandments

Exodus 20:2–17	Deuteronomy 5:6–21	A Traditional Catechetical Formula
I am the LORD your God, who brought you out of the land of Egypt, out of the house of bondage.	I am the LORD your God, who brought you out of the land of Egypt, out of the house of bondage.	1. I am the LORD your God: you shall not have strange gods before me.
You shall have no other gods before me. You shall not make for yourself a graven image, or any likeness of anything that is in heaven above, or that is in the earth beneath, or that is in the water under the earth; you shall not bow down to them or serve them; for I the LORD your God am a jealous God, visiting the iniquity of the fathers upon the children to the third and the fourth generation of those who hate me, but showing mercy to	You shall have no other gods before me. You shall not make for yourself a graven image, or any likeness of anything that is in heaven above, or that is on the earth beneath, or that is in the water under the earth; you shall not bow down to them or serve them; for I the LORD your God am a jealous God, visiting the iniquity of the fathers upon the children to the third and fourth generation of those who hate me, but showing merciful love to	

thousands of those who love me and keep my commandments.	thousands of those who love me and keep my commandments.	
You shall not take the name of the LORD your God in vain; for the LORD will not hold him guiltless who takes his name in vain.	You shall not take the name of the LORD your God in vain: for the LORD will not hold him guiltless who takes his name in vain.	2. You shall not take the name of the LORD your God in vain.
Remember the sabbath day, to keep it holy. Six days you shall labor, and do all your work; but the seventh day is a sabbath to the LORD your God; in it you shall not do any work, you, or your son, or your daughter, your manservant, or your maidservant, or your cattle, or the sojourner who is within your gates; for in six days the LORD made heaven and earth, the sea, and all that is in them, and rested the seventh day; therefore the Lord blessed the sabbath day and hallowed it.	Observe the sabbath day, to keep it holy, as the LORD your God commanded you. Six days you shall labor, and do all your work; but the seventh day is a sabbath to the LORD your God; in it you shall not do any work, you, or your son, or your daughter, or your manservant, or your maidservant, or your ox, or your donkey, or any of your cattle, or the sojourner who is within your gates, that your manservant and your maid servant may rest as well as you. You shall	3. Remember to keep holy the LORD's Day.

	remember that you were a servant in the land of Egypt, and the LORD your God brought you out from there with a might hand and an outstretched arm; therefore the LORD your God commanded you to keep the sabbath day.	
Honor your father and your mother, that your days may be long in the land which the LORD your God gives you.	Honor your father and your mother, as the LORD your God commanded you, that your days may be prolonged, and that it may go well with you, in the land which the LORD your God gives you.	4. Honor your father and your mother.
You shall not kill.	You shall not kill.	5. You shall not kill.
You shall not commit adultery.	Neither shall you commit adultery.	6. You shall not commit adultery.
You shall not steal.	Neither shall you steal.	7. You shall not steal.
You shall not bear false witness against your neighbor.	Neither shall you bear false witness against your neighbor.	8. You shall not bear false witness against your neighbor.

You shall not covet your neighbor's house; you shall not covet your neighbor's wife, or his manservant, or his maidservant, or his ox, or his donkey, or anything that is your neighbor's.

Neither shall you covet your neighbor's wife; and you shall not desire your neighbor's house, his field, or his manservant, or his maidservant, his ox, or his donkey, or anything that is your neighbor's.

9. You shall not covet your neighbor's wife.
10. You shall not covet your neighbor's goods.

The First Commandment:
No Other Gods

A while back, one of my blog readers sent me a hilarious note:

> Hey, Mark, you may get terrific questions as a Catholic author-speaker, but as a Catholic high school teacher, I get terrific answers. My current favorite:
>
> Q: Name the seven capital/deadly sins.
> A: (among the others): Sluttony.

I have to say, I enjoy this brilliant accidental coinage. Out of the mouths of babes comes a curious moral insight into our culture. It describes millions of square miles of what now constitute "Western values" (that is, the values being proposed to us by the manufacturers of culture in New York, DC, and Los Angeles as a counter narrative to the gospel and Christian virtues).

But though the insight is wonderful, it remains nonetheless accidental. We may be happy when a bad tennis player flails and accidentally wallops one over the net, but we don't thereby confuse him with a good tennis player. Similarly, this student's poor familiarity with elementary Catholic moral teaching, while luckily insightful, is still the equivalent of throwing her racquet at the ball and accidentally scoring a point. We need to do better than that in the game of life, and the quickest way to start is to learn something about the Ten Commandments.

One-quarter of the *Catechism of the Catholic Church* is devoted to the moral life, founded on the revelation given in the Ten

Commandments. (The other three-quarters is occupied by the Creed, the seven sacraments, and the Our Father.) Of course, to say that the Ten Commandments are "revealed" already raises a problem, which atheist polemicists like Christopher Hitchens have pounced on. He argued that it is silly to say the commandments are revealed because it is silly to say people did not know murder was wrong till Moses told them so on Mount Sinai.[2] Therefore, he argues, God has nothing to do with our knowledge of right and wrong.

He might have a point if Scripture itself did not record numerous tales of murder and mayhem occurring long before Mount Sinai. These make it clear that the wrongness of murder and similar grave sins was, *of course*, known since the dawn of time (otherwise the story of Cain and Abel, not to mention Moses' murder of the Egyptian, makes no sense). In other words, it is not news to the authors of Scripture that certain things are knowable by the light of natural law apart from revelation on Mount Sinai.

This is why the Church has a long history of appealing to all people of goodwill whether or not they are Catholic, Christian, or even theists, in attempting various good works such as feeding the hungry or working for peace in war-torn regions. Indeed, a core aspect of her revelation is that God is just, wise, good, and loving, and he creates us all, not just Catholics and not just Christians, in his image and likeness (Genesis 1:27). This fundamental fact of the universe is met by a variety of human responses:

• Some people admit that humans are made in God's image and likeness and try to be just, wise, good, and loving out of love for him.

• Some people admit this and try to be just, wise, good, and loving out of fear of him.

• Some people do not know this and try to be just, wise, good, and loving out of some pagan notion that the gods or karma or the Tao ordain it.

- Some people do not admit this and try to be just, wise, good, and loving out of a muddled notion that they are just that sort of chap.
- Some people do not admit this and try to be just, wise, good, and loving out of a muddled notion that their chromosomes, speaking by the holy spirit of evolution, command it.
- Some people do not admit this, say, "Who cares about trying to be just, wise, good, and loving? I don't have to listen to my chromosomes when they determine my hair color, so why should I listen to them when they say to sacrifice for the good of the species?" and do what they want.

It is not the case that an atheist must perforce be immoral. Many unbelievers choose to do what is right and are, in fact, intensely moralistic (Hitchens was among them). The problem is rather that atheists cannot account for why their morals are a thing of transcendent and universal authority (like the will of God) and not a thing of completely conditional and unbinding taste, like a preference for cheddar over American cheese. Typically, atheist attempts to give "evolutionary" explanations are a farrago of nonsense. But the important thing in the end, is that the farrago is normally marshaled by the atheist to explain why he must obey, not ignore, the moral law. That's good, and it shows that just as there is such a thing as hypocrisy—being worse than one's best rhetoric—there is also such a thing as what I call *eupocrisy*—being *better* than one's own ugly philosophy. Thus many an atheist can chatter about survival of the fittest and nature's inexorable law of weeding out the weak—but then do charitable works for the downtrodden instead of letting them starve as "unfit." As Christians we can hope that such atheists will one day find themselves saying, "Lord, when did we see you hungry…, thirsty…, naked…, sick or in prison?" and hear in reply, "Truly, I say to you, as you did it to one of the least of these my brethren, you did it to me" (Matthew 25:37–40).

That said, it absolutely remains the case that a materialist atheist cannot supply a coherent account of *why* he is moral, nor even how he knows what good and evil are, without smuggling in transcendent categories that are stolen from natural law (which is ultimately from God, the inventor of nature) or Judeo-Christian revelation. As the *real* modern atheist, philosopher Richard Rorty, pointed out, apart from reliance on God, there *is* no universally valid answer to moral questions such as "Why not be cruel?" Said Rorty:

> Anybody who thinks that there are well-grounded theoretical answers to this sort of question…is still, in his heart, a theologian or a metaphysician. He believes in an order beyond time and change which both determines the point of human existence and establishes a hierarchy of responsibilities.[3]

It is to avoid admitting this fact (even to themselves) that intensely moralistic atheists such as Hitchens or Richard Dawkins concoct claptrap about "selfish genes" nobody has ever seen to "explain" the "real" source of his moral intuitions. The notion is that these genes no one has ever discovered magically impel us to be moral so as to preserve the gene pool—with no explanation as to why we should (note that word) obey such genes but are under no obligation to obey the genes that dictate our hair color. All this is nothing other than an effort to paper over the fact that atheist morality basically consists of theft of bits and pieces from what God has revealed through nature and revelation. I have no objection to the theft. It's what keeps atheists in possession of what sanity they have. But theft it remains.

The irony of the "new atheism" is how extremely old it is. Though it is presently marketed as the New Hotness, the reality is that the only two arguments that have ever existed for atheism were already old as dirt by the time the first books of the Old Testament were being written. Those arguments are summarized thus by St. Thomas:

Objection 1: It seems that God does not exist, because if one of two contraries be infinite, the other would be altogether destroyed. But the word "God" means that he is infinite goodness. If, therefore, God existed, there would be no evil discoverable; but there is evil in the world. Therefore God does not exist.

(Translation: Bad things happen, so there's no God.)

and

Objection 2: Further, it is superfluous to suppose that what can be accounted for by a few principles has been produced by many. But it seems that everything we see in the world can be accounted for by other principles, supposing God did not exist. For all natural things can be reduced to one principle which is nature; and all voluntary things can be reduced to one principle which is human reason, or will. Therefore there is no need to suppose God's existence.

(Translation: Everything seems to work fine without God, so there's no God.)

It takes a species of modest intelligence about ten seconds for one or both of these ideas to occur to it in a world like ours, especially in an age without anesthetics. Consequently, the psalmist already contends with those who say there is no God (Psalm 14:1). And once it has occurred to a human being to propose the rejection of God, we then discover the truth of the old aphorism that when people stop believing in God, they don't believe in nothing: they believe in anything.

In the Old Testament, the "anything" people believed in ranged from dung beetles to milk cows in a vast pantheon of nature deities represented by sundry idols. The choice, then as now, was stark: Worship God or worship something made by God. There was no third option. And Israel, who worshiped God (in fits and starts) had a jolly time making raspberries at Team Pagan over the implications of idol worship:

> Not to us, O LORD, not to us,
>   but to your name give glory,
>   for the sake of thy steadfast love and thy faithfulness!
> Why should the nations say,
>   "Where is their God?"
> Our God is in the heavens;
>   he does whatever he pleases.
> Their idols are silver and gold,
>   The work of men's hands.
> They have mouths, but do not speak;
>   eyes, but do not see.
> They have ears, but do not hear;
>   noses, but do not smell.
> They have hands, but do not feel;
>   feet, but do not walk;
>   and they do not make a sound in their throat.
> Those who make them are like them;
>   so are all who trust in them.
>
> O Israel, trust in the LORD!
>   He is their help and their shield. (Psalm 115:1–9)

A modern reader sees this as ugly triumphalism, but a modern reader needs to remember that at the time this was written, the Jewish conception of God was by no means a triumph. Jews, the sole champions on planet Earth of belief in a Transcendent God beyond all time and space, were a tiny beleaguered nation squeezed and battered by every pagan empire from Egypt to Assyria to Babylon to Persia to Greece to Rome. They emphatically saw themselves as the little underdogs beaten up by the Big Established Powers. So if you really want to get the hang of how such mockery of pagan idolatry felt to the psalmist and his audience, don't imagine a well-fed American Evangelical finding a dreadlocked Renaissance Faire pagan (complete with "I Heart Gandalf" sticker on his VW bus) and holding him up for public ridicule on some *Morning Gospel Hour Show*. Imagine instead Groucho Marx poking fun at some sneering plutocrat in a top hat and monocle. The whole world and all the Best People were pagan nature-worshipers when the psalmist wrote that lampoon. People who said that God utterly transcended nature were the kooky minority.

And as the West returns to paganism in our post-Christian age, it again returns to nature worship and is again faced with exactly the same problems that confronted idol worshipers five thousand years ago—again with no third option. For an atheist materialist now cannot, any more than an ancient pagan could then, give a coherent account of the *why* of his morality because one cannot derive *ought* from *is* now any more than one could five thousand years ago. In the end, the modern materialist's failure is exactly the same failure as the pagans of old because, in the end, he worships—as they did—the creature instead of the Creator. To be sure, the modern materialist does not make quite so crude a mistake as the worshipper of false gods the psalmist lampooned. He may not worship a statue or a rock with the rites and oblations of an ancient pagan. But, in the end, he does indeed worship a creature. Sometimes, the idol may be the big rock called "Earth" (generally worshiped under the title "the environment" when proposed as an alternative to God). Very often the object of worship is the three pound piece of meat behind the atheist's own eyes, hailed under the Trinitarian name of Science, Intellect, and Reason.

The problem with that god and that creed is this: Science can tell you how much Hitler weighed and how much carbon was in Mother Teresa's body. But it cannot tell you, in the slightest, why we should prefer the morality of the one over the other. Every "scientific" attempt to do so is smuggling in moral imperatives such as "Life is preferable to death" and "People should be loved, not murdered," which are ultimately derived from the fact that people are made in the image and likeness of God. Anyone who claims to "scientifically" prove that a human being is more valuable than a housefly is practicing sleight of hand and self-deception. You cannot heat a man on a Bunsen burner until he releases the blue and gold gasses of human dignity. We know of such things, not from science, but from natural law and revelation—the twin gifts of the God who made us in his image and likeness. Both the theist and the atheist receive and use those gifts, but the atheist does so without saying "thank you." The result of this ingratitude is a reductionist philosophy that tells us the only real things are time, space, matter, and energy whirling through a mindless void—a philosophy too small to account for the philosopher.

And that brings us back to why we speak of the commandments as "revealed." The Church is perfectly aware that some of the commandments encapsulate moral truths knowable by the light of natural law. But taken as a whole, the effect of the commandments is to root our natural moral perceptions in supernatural revelation. The commandments are therefore not primarily about setting up an ethical arrangement for a functioning civil order. Rather, the point of the Ten Commandments—and above all of the first commandment—is to root the natural moral law in God, the Author of the human person and to call Israel (and ultimately the whole human race) into a relationship with him. That is why the commandments are ordered the way they are. The first commandment speaks to Israel not in the language of philosophy but in the language of *covenant*:

> I am the LORD your God, who brought you out of the land
> of Egypt, out of the house of bondage.
> You shall have no other gods before me. (Exodus 20:2–3)

Perhaps the most significant word in this passage is *your*. Without it, there is no covenant, for it is in God's giving himself to us (and we to him) that a covenant—a sacred family bond of kinship—happens.

"The Lord God" is a remote deity, somewhere up in heaven. He is powerful, to be sure, and the artificer of the universe, but still remote. But "the Lord *your* God," though still awesome and powerful and the Maker of all, is something more: a personal God who gives himself to us and who calls us to give ourselves to him unreservedly and with complete devotion, as he has done.

This will matter in considering all the rest of the commandments. For the Ten Commandments reveal the moral law to be not the product of accidental natural selection with the sole purpose of protecting the gene pool, nor the product of an impersonal Tao, nor something of human origin, but an expression of God's love for us. This love is fully revealed not on Sinai but on Golgotha.

The 1.5 Commandment
Concerning Images

One tricky thing about the commandments is figuring out how to break them up. The original Hebrew text refers to them as (pedantry alert!) the "Ten Words" but doesn't do all that tidy stuff with the Roman numerals clearly delineating where one commandment leaves off and another starts. As a result, you have to make a judgment call about whether you will (1) divide the first commandment into two—one about worshiping God alone and the other forbidding the worship of graven images—or (2) divide the last one into two commandments about coveting your neighbor's wife and coveting your neighbor's stuff.

Some of our Protestant brethren have dark visions of Catholics tunneling under their houses because of all this, as illustrated by this common sight on the Internet:[4]

Bible Ten Commandments	Catholic Ten Commandments
I am the Lord thy God, which have brought thee out of the land of Egypt, out of the house of bondage. Thou shalt have no other gods before me.	I am the Lord thy God. Thou shalt have no strange gods before Me.

Exodus 20:4–6	
You shall not make for yourself an idol in the form of anything in heaven above or on the earth beneath or in the waters below. You shall not bow down to them or worship them; for I, the LORD your God, am a jealous God, punishing the children for the sin of the fathers to the third and fourth generation of those who hate me, but showing love to a thousand genera-tions of those who love me and keep my Commandments.	Deleted. See also idolatry in the Catholic Church (There is idolatry in the papal system so the second Commandment has been deleted or sometimes it has been absorbed into the first. All remaining Commandments are therefore shifted along one count.)

Yet a brief glance at the *Catechism of the Catholic Church* or any Catholic Bible dispels the notion that anything has been deleted. It's all there, safe and sound:

Article 1
The First Commandment
I am the LORD your God, who brought you out of the land of Egypt, out of the house of bondage. You shall have no other gods before me. You shall not make for yourself a graven image, or any likeness of anything that is in heaven above, or that is in the earth beneath, or that is in the water under the earth; you shall not bow down to them or serve them. (*CCC*, 2083, quoting Exodus 20:2–5; see Deuteronomy 5:6–9)

So the conspiracy theorist above is inaccurate about what Catholics are up to in their Bibles and Catechisms, but many still find themselves stumped by the apparent contradiction between the command-ment and their lived experience. If graven images are forbidden by God, then what's up with that Mary statue and the crucifix in the sanctuary?

It's a reasonable question. But it's also worth noting that those who ask it expend almost all their energy *solely* on the Mary statue and the crucifix, while paying no attention whatsoever to their own bowling trophies, family photo albums, Precious Feet pins, or change in their pockets. All these things are likenesses of things in heaven above, earth beneath, and water under the earth too. Some of them, like the bowling trophy, are even genuine graven images.

But these images don't typically count because they are either not churchy, religiony images or they are the *right kind* of churchy religiony images, acceptable in evangelical and fundamentalist circles. So, for instance, many non-Catholic churches refuse to display a crucifix, since the body of Jesus on the crucifix is, well, an image of the body of Jesus, and images of anything in heaven above, or in the earth beneath, or in the water under the earth are supposedly bad. So instead a bare cross is placed in the sanctuary, and nobody seems to realize that a bare cross is an *image*—of the cross!

Also overlooked in all this inconsistent hubbub is the fact that God himself, just a few chapters after he gives the prohibition against images, tells Moses how he wants him to adorn the mercy seat which will form the lid of the ark of the covenant, the holiest object in all of the Jewish tradition:

> And you shall make two cherubim of gold; of hammered work shall you make them, on the two ends of the mercy seat. Make one cherub on the one end, and one cherub on the other end; of one piece with the mercy seat shall you make the cherubim on its two ends. The cherubim shall spread out their wings above, overshadowing the mercy seat with their

wings, their faces one to another; toward the mercy seat shall the faces of the cherubim be. (Exodus 25:18–20)

In other words, the God who seemingly forbids all images almost immediately commands the Israelites to make an image—*and put it on their holiest object.* What gives?

What gives is the prohibition of idolatry, not of imagery. Old Testament piety is absolute in barring Israel from acting like pagans and worshiping creatures—including the amazingly easy-to-worship work of one's own hands. (Indeed, as pagan myths like Pygmalion and modern phenomena like workaholism show, it is amazingly easy to fall in love with and give your life over to the service of the work of your own hands.) The temptation is to confuse things that remind us of God with God himself. And so pagan antiquity worshiped a whole host of creatures (as does modern post-Christian paganism, with its particularly strong adoration of the Golden Calf of money, sex, and power).

But as the images of the cherubim on the ark of the covenant attest, it is quite possible to have images that are not objects of worship but instead point us to him who alone must be worshiped. That was the silent message of the cherubim as they faced one another on the mercy seat atop the ark of the covenant, bowing in adoration of the invisible God. It was a sharp but undeniable foreshadow of when God would take flesh and *become* an image himself.

C.S. Lewis remarks of Israel that it was the destiny of that nation to be turned from the likeness to the Reality. And so all short cuts (like physical images) were denied them by this commandment. They were being prepared not for the revelation of a God without an image but for the revelation of Jesus, who is the true "image of the invisible God" (Colossians 1:15). When that image came and God stamped his likeness on the human face of Jesus, the prohibition was transfigured.

That is why Catholics can have statues and icons while retaining this commandment in our Bibles. It is still true that no creaturely image can be adored as a god. But it is also true that images are a participation in the light of God, shining through the incarnate image of God who is Jesus Christ. Saints, who are members of Christ's body, are now windows into God, not barriers to his light or the cheap Brand-X substitutes for his glory known as idols. Therefore, in honoring (not worshiping) their images, we honor (not worship) the saints they represent. And in honoring the saints, we honor their Lord, who is the true image of God.

CHAPTER TWO

The Second Commandment
Hallow God's Name

Exodus is the Greek name for the second book of the Bible. In Hebrew it is called the Book of Names. That's because, like Catholic encyclicals, the Hebrew books of the Bible are titled by the opening words of the book. And Exodus begins, "These are the names…"

It is fitting that this title be given to Exodus, since Exodus is a book in which names play a huge role, in both the way they are emphasized and the way they are strategically deemphasized. Exodus pauses to tell us the names of the two earliest pro-life heroines, Shiphrah and Puah, who saved Moses and other Hebrew boys from the clutches of the masterminds of the First Cairo Population Control Conference (see Exodus 1:15–20) who said, like modern population planners, "Just enough of me. Way too much of you." Exodus 2:10 tells us how Moses got his name—a pun on the phrase "to draw out," which owes to his being drawn out of the Nile and which also prophesies his role in drawing Israel out of Egypt. The book even disses the villain of the piece, the most powerful man on the planet at that time, by steadfastly refusing to name him anything other than "Pharaoh."

But the most important name comes in Exodus 3—the divine name. When the voice speaks from the burning bush and Moses rather reluctantly answers, a perfectly Jewish conversation full of wordplay and dickering takes place. What is striking about it all is how Moses manages to combine reverence and awe in the divine presence that created him with a certain audacity. He asks for proof (as if the voice from the burning bush is not enough). He wheedles and cajoles and begs to be excused. He talks God into making his brother Aaron the spokesman. And in the end he asks, "Whom shall I say sent me?"

It is a question pregnant with a significance lost on us, because we do not understand what names meant to the ancient Hebrew mind. To them, the name was a deeply sacred thing. It was not just a label slapped on a thing so that one could call it something besides a thing-amajig. A person's name expressed their essence.

So in Scripture we repeatedly find names imbued with huge significance as a sort of key to the person's inmost being. Isaac means "laughter," and he springs from the laughter of his incredulous and joyful parents as the long-delayed promise of a son is wonderfully fulfilled (see Genesis 21:3–7). Jacob's name means "deceiver," and he rips off his brother's birthright and cheats his father-in-law out of livestock (Genesis 27; 30:25–43). And when God changes Jacob's name to "Israel" this too is true as the deceptive Jacob is transformed over time into he who has "striven with God" (Genesis 32:28).

In other words, to know someone's name was to know him or her. To name, or rename, someone was to effect and reflect a fundamental change in who the person was. So when God reveals his name, he is revealing *himself*.

We experience a tiny glimpse of that intimacy when some figure we have known or revered as an august adult presence ("Mr. Smith, the math professor") turns to us and says, "Call me Jim." We sense it in a negative way when somebody who should know our name forgets it. It's hard to escape the sense that they have forgotten *us*.

The Covenant Relationship

God's revelation of his name is, therefore, an invitation to intimacy. It is also a profound revelation of who he is. Other names given to God in Scripture are basically titles that tell us some of his attributes. But "I AM WHO I AM" tells us who God is in his essence: the Self-Existent One (Exodus 3:14). God does not have to reveal his name, and Moses certainly has no power to make him do so. Yet God does so anyway out of sheer gratuitous love, and in so doing, he enters into a relationship with Moses and Israel whereby his people can call on his name.

Indeed, that's the entire point of God's revelation to Moses at the burning bush. God's purpose, which will not be thwarted, is to bring Israel not merely *out* of Egypt but *into* a covenant relationship with him at Mount Sinai. As we have already noted, a covenant is more than a contract; it is a bond of sacred kinship. Therefore, to make a covenant is to become family. So when God reveals his name to Israel, he is permitting the nation to call upon him as friend, ally, and protector.

This is a very significant step in a long process of graciously making himself vulnerable. It will ultimately lead to scourging, a crown of thorns, a buzzing cloud of flies around his naked and beaten body, and the sound of mocking taunts in his ears as he struggles for breath against the excruciating bolts of pain in his wrists and feet. Sinai is a major step forward in the drama, but it won't really be over until the redemption wrought in Christ brings the last redeemed soul into heaven.

Because Sinai is a provisional covenant pointing forward to the new and eternal covenant in Christ, certain cautions must apply. God is making a covenant with a desperately dangerous species who will misuse every good gift he gives them, including the gift of his name. So he commands: "You shall not take the name of the LORD your God in vain; for the LORD will not hold him guiltless who takes his name in vain" (Exodus 20:7).

To use the name of God is a solemn thing, not to be taken lightly. To swear in his name falsely is to call Truth himself as a witness to a lie. To invoke the name in a curse against the innocent is to call him who is Justice to be unjust and him who is Life to be death. Scripture is adamant that to do this is an extremely dangerous violation of the covenant.

Likewise, to treat the divine name as a sort of lucky rabbit's foot or abracadabra is to gravely insult the covenant, because God is God and not a genie who must make us rich or beat up our enemies at the service of our fleshly desires. He gives us the divine name so that we may *know* him. He will not let us use it to make him a bellhop for our pride, envy, anger, greed, sloth, gluttony, or lust.

Blasphemy Depends Upon the Sacred

These days, of course, the names of God and Jesus are taken lightly every day. Much of this is inculpable, since many people have not the slightest idea that they are involved in a covenant with God (assuming they are baptized). On the other hand, as some sectors become more aggressively hostile to God, there are silly initiatives such as the recent Blasphemy Challenge, in which some Internet atheists urge their fan base to blaspheme and challenge God to strike them dead for doing so. What things like this illustrate is that the Western mind can't help but live in constant debt to the God of Israel. For when Westerners blaspheme, it's always the God of Israel they blaspheme and not Zeus, Quetzalcoatl, or Athena.

Here again we see that atheism, even in blaspheming, profoundly relies on ideas stolen from revelation. The blasphemer protests that God threatens his dignity as a person—never realizing that "personhood" is a concept invented by Christian theologians. The blasphemer feels the need to assert his individuality against the oppressive dictates of a nonexistent sky god—never realizing that one of the "dictates" of God is that the self is a good thing, while it is Buddhism, not Christianity, that says the goal of life is to annihilate the self. The blasphemer wants to assert the glories of sex against the God who said, "Be fruitful and multiply," not against the gnostic demiurge who says sex is evil.

This is not to say that there is *nothing* sacred to your garden-variety Internet blasphemer. For instance, racial equality is a sacred thing; that's why he doesn't say the "N" word. The family retains some vestigial holiness, as do children. That's why pedophilia and incest are still condemned and the crimes of Christian clerics are brandished to attack the gospel. And the poor and homeless retain a certain sanctity due to the lingering cultural influence of the Defender of the widow, the orphan, and the stranger (see Deuteronomy 10:18). That's why we do not admire those who laugh at their plight.

But our culture does increasingly admire those who laugh at God. The comedy (and the tragedy) of this is that the creators of the Blasphemy Challenge actually imagine they commit an act of *courage*. Invariably, they posture as though Christians will lynch them for their brave insults to God, or the irritable old gentleman in the white beard will finally lose his temper and start throwing thunderbolts. Not knowing the first thing about the One they blaspheme, they have no idea what they are talking about.

What such people don't get is that blasphemy, like all sin, *is its own punishment*. It darkens the intellect, hardens the heart, and further disorders the appetites. The result, as Jesus says, is that "from him who has not, even what he has will be taken away" (Matthew 13:12). In this case it means that a culture that blasphemes God is a culture that will soon sacrifice its lesser sanctities as well.

That's because a culture of blasphemy ultimately has no defenses that can ensure permanent moral values. The generation that revels in shocking its parents' bourgeois devotion to God today will discover that its sons and daughters will gleefully shock its bourgeois devotion to children or racial equality tomorrow. A culture of blasphemy will continue to "push the envelope" of transgression in more and ever more attempts to stab its deadened nerves back to life. It will laugh with relief today because the Old Man on the Cloud turns out not to be so scary, and it will continue "transgressing" by committing more and more outrages against fresh "taboos" tomorrow.

Don't believe it?

• The BBC recently ran a gooey sympathy piece on a brother and sister in Germany and their "forbidden love." So incest is already on the table.[5]

• NAMBLA (the North American Man/Boy Love Association) is making pleas for civil recognition of pedophilia as a legitimate "sexual orientation." (Who can forbid two people from loving each other? The ancient Greeks saw it as a way of mentoring young boys. It just takes some getting used to…)

• CBS's *60 Minutes* pioneered snuff TV a few years ago by showing Jack Kevorkian offing a victim, while *24* glamorized torture chic as it depicted the hero fighting bad guys with Gestapo tactics in the name of America and apple pie. It was, natch, promoted as "daring" fare.

Each fresh transgressive thrill demands something a bit tangier next time. Perhaps the day is coming when folks will watch live executions and gladiatorial combat on TV. For in the end the food of blasphemy is bread and circuses. A culture that despises the sacredness of him who is beauty, truth, and sacrificial love will eventually despise the sacredness of everything we currently take as self-evidently good and decent.

Blasphemy, like all sin, cuts a culture off from love and delivers only cheap thrills that leave us starving for true life. It makes the universe a cold, dead place. The apotheosis of this is the loneliness and coldness of hell. This is not some place God "sends" people because he's a vain popinjay ticked about affronts to his ego. It's a place to which people exile themselves because, despite God's every attempt to love them (including taking a scourge, a crown of thorns, three nails, and a lance for them), they remain the pathetic sort of people who prefer to scrawl obscenities on the bathroom wall and congratulate themselves for their "courage." Worship enlarges the soul; blasphemy makes it utterly small.

The sacredness of the name is therefore not an ancient superstition. The warning still holds, and the judgment still obtains. The judgment on a culture that takes God's name lightly is that it becomes a lightweight culture, fit only to be taken lightly, as the Blasphemy Challengers so emphatically are. Today take God's name seriously, as he takes you seriously. You can do that in two simple but powerful ways. The first is to honor God's name by worshiping him in the sacrifice of the Mass, where the greatest act of honor to God's name conceivable is done as the Son offers himself eternally to the Father in love and we offer ourselves as living sacrifices to the Father in and through Jesus. There is no greater way than that to hallow God's name and keep it holy.

In addition, we can make our act of worship an act of reparation for all the insults given to God's name. Jesus himself did this on Calvary when he took all the insults and blasphemies heaped upon him and said, "Father, forgive them; for they know not what they do" (Luke 23:34). We can likewise ask that even the blasphemies of the enemies of God, the cries of anguish, the confusion of the mind of fallen man, the despair, the hopelessness, the pain, and the rage of a fallen world be turned into life, blessing, peace and hope by Christ crucified and risen. That is what the Mass is all about and that is what Jesus has been doing for two thousand years. Today is the day he wants to do it through you.

CHAPTER THREE

The Third Commandment
Honor the Sabbath

Some time ago a bumper sticker appeared urging "Support your labor union: The people who brought you the weekend." The folks who dreamed up the ad campaign seem never to have heard of the third commandment. For, of course, it was God who invented the weekend.

For the ancient pagan slave, life was work—always—except for the feast day now and then. Only those strange Jews had this glorious insistence that every seventh day must be dedicated to God in rest, contemplation, and family jollification—and this included even the "manservant" and the "maidservant" (Exodus 20:10).

What a lot of people don't know is why the Jews celebrated the Sabbath, even though Scripture is really pretty plain: The Sabbath was observed in honor of the seventh day of Creation, the day God "rested" (see Genesis 2:2–3; Exodus 20:8–11).

It's a curious thing to speak of God resting. It should be a dead giveaway that the Creation account in Genesis is not intended to be read as a newspaper but as a theological document that is getting at truths about God and our relationship with him. We need no more believe in six literal twenty-four–hour days of Creation than we need to believe that God—panting and sweating after hurling the galaxies into being and fashioning the aardvark, scarab beetle, and Eve's left eye—on the seventh day flopped down on the heavenly sofa with a brewski and took a breather.

So what's the theological point of a Sabbath rest?

To get at it, you need to know what *Sabbath* links together in the

26

ancient Hebrew mind. The words for "Sabbath" and "seven" (*shevah*) are related. They are words of covenant and oath making, for to make a covenant is to swear an oath, and in Hebrew, to swear an oath is to "seven yourself."

The author of Genesis tells the story of Creation in a deeply *liturgical* way. He portrays the earth as a sort of temple or tabernacle, where all is ordered toward the worship of God. And just as a pagan shrine always had at its heart an image of a god, so the Creation account zeros in on an image as well: man and woman, the image and likeness of God himself.

The point is profoundly subversive of pagan thinking. The image of the God of Israel is, like the pagan image, made of the clay of the earth (*adamah*). But instead of the king or some other poobah having sole contact with the god, Israel's God is reflected in the lowest plowboy and slave. Yet the true God is not to be identified with any of the creatures worshiped by the nations. They are his creation, not his embodiment. Earth is his footstool, not his vesture.

In the same way the scriptural portrayal of the Sabbath is deeply liturgical. It is a sort of sanctuary in time, just as the tabernacle and temple were sanctuaries in space. The Sabbath was a sign, every seventh day, that creation is ordered toward God and finds its rest in him. Not surprisingly then, when the covenant relationship of God and man takes a giant step forward at Sinai, God reiterates the great sign of the covenant by commanding Israel, "Remember the sabbath day, to keep it holy" (Exodus 20:8).

It is commonly noted that the Church "changed the Sabbath from Saturday to Sunday," but strictly speaking this is not so. The truth is, the real Sabbath was never a day of the week any more than the real Lamb of God was a member of the species *Ovis aries*. On the contrary, the real Sabbath, like the real Lamb of God, is Jesus Christ, who is our rest.

The Old Testament Sabbath was not simply a sign that pointed backward to the covenant in Creation. It was also a prophetic foreshadowing of the Messiah, who would bring true rest and deliver us into the ultimate Promised Land, heaven. That is the point of the somewhat obscure language of Hebrews 4, which urges Jewish Christians—who are tempted to return to the old covenant—to enter into a new sort of Sabbath rest via the new covenant of Christ. Something more than the seventh day of the week is needed for the true Sabbath rest. That something is not Sunday but Jesus.

Paul states this elsewhere:

> Therefore let no one pass judgment on you in questions of food and drink or with regard to a festival or a new moon or a sabbath. These are only a shadow of what is to come; but the substance belongs to Christ (Colossians 2:16).

That doesn't mean, "Don't observe the Lord's Day." It means that the Church observes the Lord's Day as a way of sacramentally realizing the grace of Christ in time, just as she realizes the grace of Christ in matter through the sacraments. The reason that happens on Sunday and not Saturday is because Sunday is the eighth day of Creation, the day of the Resurrection of Jesus, who is the sign of the new covenant. This is, by the way, not a change that came in the Dark Ages; it was already recognized in the first century. John, in Revelation 1:10, prefaces his vision by telling us, "I was in the Spirit *on the Lord's day*" (emphasis added). He means, "I was at Mass. It was Sunday." In this, he accords with the tradition of the Gospel writers. Whenever they mention a day of the week for a resurrection appearance of Jesus, it is invariably a Sunday.

The cool thing about the Sabbath rest who is Christ is that he continues all the best parts of the old observation of the Sabbath. The Church still calls us out of the rat race and bids us to remember that the real story of our lives is not "work, buy, consume, die" but "pray and play." She can do this because a basic message of the gospel is that everything—including work—is a gratuitous gift. The Church that long ago told slaves that they were the equals of their masters, that they were human beings and not talking plows, and that life is a gift to be received with gratitude before it is a struggle to be fought, still tells us that the first and last word in life is *Eucharist*—"thanksgiving"—not survival of the fittest.

Bill Gates once said, "Just in terms of allocation of time resources, religion is not very efficient. There's a lot more I could be doing on a Sunday morning."[6] The Sabbath is here to remind us that there is something fundamentally irrational about this kind of cold money-driven rationalism, something fundamentally illogical about being merely logical. It whispers that the bottom line isn't the bottom line, and we are being wildly wasteful if we are trying to be merely economical. For there is in the very idea of Creation something extravagant, artistic, and playful. God, after all, didn't have to create anything. He was under no economic necessity, and he has never been constrained by worries about allocations of time resources or efficiency. Creation, says Robert Farrar Capon, is "radically unnecessary."[7]

There is only one explanation for Creation: God creates for love. He creates just because he wants to. He creates as an artist creates, not as a production engineer creates. He creates because creation is a lovely thing, not because creation is a necessary thing. And we, who are made in his image, are missing the point of the whole extravagant show if we focus exclusively on economics or the machinery of government and never get it into our hearts that these are no more the central story of existence than the cost of paint is the central story of the Sistine Chapel ceiling.

Not that work during the rest of the week doesn't matter, mind you. It does. But it matters because of us, not we because of it. For we too are not necessary: We exist because God loves us and thought it would be fun to have us around. Therefore work is dignified because we do it. But so is play.

Some people think play is just stuff we do when we aren't doing *real* things, like work. In reality, both work and play are made real by us, who are the only things, says the Church, that God has created for our own sakes (see *CCC*, 1703). This means, among other things, that there is a real place for delight in sheer play—in games, in songs, in baseball and in lemonade and in that sunny day peeping in the school window over the shoulder of our grim economics tutor.

So we honor the Sabbath by, of course, worshiping God at Mass. But we also do well to honor it by being a little silly and savoring the goodness of his work in Creation and redemption. So do your homework, be responsible, and attend to business. But remember that the ultimate business of life is joy, for as C.S. Lewis once said, "Joy is the serious business of heaven."[8]

This is a classic example of the way in which holiness and merriment are bound up together. Holidays come from holy days.

CHAPTER FOUR

The Fourth Commandment
Honor Your Father and Mother

With the fourth commandment ("Honor your father and your mother, that your days may be long in the land which the LORD your God gives you" [Exodus 20:12]), we enter into territory that is closer to what we call "natural law." Basically, this command is one of those things knowable to anybody with a pulse. It is (or would seem to be) up there with stuff like "Don't murder." It's one of those things that even pagan piety speaks of highly. And so here again many moderns ask the same question as Christopher Hitchens: What is the point of God commanding something that any person of common sense knows to be right?

It's a fairly potent question—as long as we speak of family in the abstract. If all families were like the Cleavers or the Huxtables, it would be a snap to honor your father and mother. But when we look at, for instance, the R-rated story of the Old Testament family (and quite possibly of our own family), the reason the fourth commandment is a *commandment* comes into clearer focus.

The bottom line is this: God doesn't *command* us to obey the law of gravity. Why not? Because we will obey it, whether we like it or not. But in the case of the natural law commandments of the Decalogue, we retain the element of choice—and therefore the possibility of sin and virtue. As free creatures we have it in us to *not* honor our father and mother. Moreover, as fallen creatures subject to temptation, there will be moments when what appears to be easy and natural suddenly becomes a radical challenge.

So if Dad comes home three sheets to the wind for the umpteenth time, or Mom ditches Dad, you, and the siblings to take up with her personal trainer and (as she writes in the farewell e-mail) "do what I need to do for me," well, that's when the command to honor your father and mother gets a severe test.

Similarly, all the little aggravations of domestic life can pile up: that story Dad always tells guests about the stupid thing you did when you were nine; Grandma's racist hissing about the neighbors; Dad's farting in front of the guy you are trying to impress on your first date and then (cringe) drawing even more attention to it with lame jokes about barking spiders. Then there's the chintziness, the small-mindedness, the bullying, the neglect, the violence—all the various ways in which our parents can make us wish we were adopted. These and a million other things can make the obviousness of the fourth commandment fade into the void.

That's why this is a *commandment*. It acts as a sort of anchor to say, "Yes, it's tempting to toss the old goat overboard right now. But stop. Cool off. Remember your sacred obligation."

Dishonorable Elders

Some chalk this commandment up to the mere domination of strong over weak that underlay a lot of Bronze Age (and modern-day) culture. But that is a very simplistic reading of Scripture. In fact, the Old Testament, even as it enshrines this commandment as one of the Big Ten, does not hesitate to offer some very harsh critiques of a great many parental figures. Indeed, the Jewish tradition (and the Christian tradition following it) manages to couple the command to honor your father and mother with some of the most vociferous (and unique) criticism of elders in the ancient world. Where pagan literature is all about the glories of the king who is father to his people, his most favored monarch status with the gods, and his inexorable power, Hebrew Scripture is full to bursting with frank assessments of kings who, for the most part, "did what was evil in the eyes of the LORD." Then there are constant declarations that "our fathers" did what was wicked and were justly punished for it. It is fair to say that, virtually alone in the ancient world, the Jews invented the entire genre of penitent, self-critical literature and practiced the most withering form of raw and brutal self-assessment of their national failings—and those of their ancestors.

This does not stop with the birth of the new covenant. Jesus speaks as a typical Jewish prophet when he blasts the *elders* in Jerusalem with:

> Woe to you, scribes and Pharisees, hypocrites! for you build the tombs of the prophets and adorn the monuments of the righteous, saying, "If we had lived in the days of our fathers, we would not have taken part with them in shedding the blood of the prophets." Thus you witness against yourselves, that you are sons of those who murdered the prophets. Fill up, then, the measure of your fathers. You serpents, you brood of vipers, how are you to escape being sentenced to hell? Therefore I send you prophets and wise men and scribes, some of whom you will kill and crucify, and some you will scourge in your synagogues and persecute from town to town, that upon you may come all the righteous blood shed on earth, from the blood of innocent Abel to the blood of Zechariah the son of Barachiah, whom you murdered between the sanctuary and the altar. (Matthew 23:29–35)

Note, once again, the typical habit of the Hebrew prophet in linking the sins of father and son, not so much by blood as by the fact that they make the same sinful choices. Indeed, Jesus' cavalier disregard for connections of blood was famous—and infamous to his detractors. He replies to typical florid Near Eastern flattery about the blessedness of the mother who bore him and nursed him with, "Blessed rather are those who hear the word of God and keep it!" (Luke 11:28). Still more shocking to first-century family values, he declares, "If any one comes to me and does not hate his own father and mother and wife and children and brothers and sisters, yes, and even his own life, he cannot be my disciple" (Luke 14:26).

Put yourself in the shoes of an average Jew of the time, and listen to the Master:

> Do not think that I have come to bring peace on earth; I have not come to bring peace, but a sword. For I have come to set a man against his father, and a daughter against her mother, and a daughter-in-law against her mother-in-law; and a man's foes will be those of his own household. He who loves father or mother more than me is not worthy of me; and he who loves son or daughter more than me is not worthy of me. (Matthew 10:34–37)

Would you entrust your daughter to a church whose pastor spoke those words? Many of Jesus' contemporaries regarded him as a manifest enemy of the family. And yet, paradoxically, nothing else in the history of the world has been a greater friend of the family and the hearth than the Church Christ founded. What is the answer to this riddle?

It is found in Jesus' own remarks about dying to self to find life. A culture that raises family and the ties of blood to the supreme good is a culture that cannot get past tribal allegiances. This was the great stumbling block of the Jews: Jesus accepted the wrong sort of people. Not just prostitutes and tax collectors and such riffraff, but *foreigners*: Samaritan half-breeds, Syro-Phoenician dogs, and even Roman thugs whose oppression, murder, and raiding of the public kitty had long ago worn out their welcome. The notion that these awful outsiders and aliens could somehow be chosen right along with Israel was more than many could take. For the Jews who rejected Jesus and his apostles, the ties of blood wound up trumping God's choice to include the whole human race in his covenant family.

And yet, the covenant family was to include us all, and the Church is the living proof. The supernatural family of the covenant has expanded to include anybody who would accept baptism: some 1.2 billion people and climbing. That's what *Catholic* means: universal.

The Christian picture is not "Honor your parents" *versus* "Honor God" but rather "Honor God first" *followed by* "Honor your parents." Seek first the things of earth—even a happy family—and that will all be lost in the end. For this world is a passing world. Seek first his kingdom and his righteousness, and everything else—including a healthy family life—will be added to you as well.

Modern Dilemmas

Of course, the challenge to honor one's parents goes on through all generations, and my generation has not done a bang-up job. As the most narcissistic and self-absorbed generation in human history, we Baby Boomers are slowly discovering that the Christian revelation is a description of the way things *are*, not of the way we wish things were. So that little tag on the fourth commandment—"that your days may be long in the land which the LORD your God gives you"—is not a threat so much as a product warning label placed on the human person by the Manufacturer. Ignore it at your peril, just as you ignore the "Don't use in the shower" label on your hair dryer at your peril.

We clever Boomers set about reinventing everything from culture to religion to sex in the confident assurance that we could do it right and that fathers and mothers of countless generations past were fools. We now bid fair to end by excelling our parents in one special way: by being greater fools than any other generation. Generation Narcissus, extolling itself for discovering consequence-free sex in the sixties and seventies, is also the generation that discovered such consequences as AIDS, a massive STD rate, overwhelming destruction of the family, and a staggering abortion death toll. The generation that tirelessly praised itself in the sixties for first figuring out that war is bad and mocking the generation who fought Hitler, Tojo, and the Commies ("Never trust anyone over thirty!") has ended by marching its children off to a foolish war of choice in Iraq and birthing a mushrooming complex of little wars across the globe, coupled with a metastasizing national security police state that would have horrified our grandparents. And the flower children who lectured their Depression-era parents on simplicity and getting back to the earth have brought the economies of the world to the brink of collapse with reckless self-indulgence.

Moral: We are dwarves who stand on the shoulders of giants. When we do not honor our fathers and mothers, we succeed only in creating a world where our children have nothing to honor in us. Indeed, my heart goes out to Gen X and Y as they try to rise to the challenge of honoring us, their Generation Narcissus parents. It does not surprise me at all that millions of them simply look back over their parents' heads to celebrate their grandparents in the Greatest Generation just as they also have gone in droves to hear Popes John Paul II and Benedict XVI speak. The natural desire to honor parents is abundantly present in our youth. But we Boomers have given them precious little to work with.

On the other hand, there is also the reality that kids imitate their parents. Many of the young who have survived Generation Narcissus's assault on unborn life show disturbing evidence that they have learned the key lesson we Boomers labored to teach them: Inconvenient people should be killed. When Generation Narcissus gets too old to change the Beatles CD and the children get restless and impatient with their self-absorbed and increasingly demanding parents, that lesson will, I fear, be acted upon. The euthanasia movement is birthing a world in which all our improvements upon the Ten Commandments will come home to roost as we Boomers become expensive—and defenseless.

The remedy for this sundering of the natural affections between parents and children, as it is for all other forms of sin, is hard and simple: Repent, and believe the Good News, that God may "turn the hearts of fathers to their children and the hearts of children to their fathers" (Malachi 4:6). And that remedy is, in fact, taken up again with each generation. So, for instance, we see such movements as the Militia Immaculata continuing the work begun by St. Maximilian Kolbe. The great saint, martyred at Auschwitz during World War II, sought to increase the honor given to the greatest mother of all: the Blessed Virgin Mary. He had a great love for young people and his mission in the United States is now based at Marytown near Chicago. The Militia Immaculata are taking up the challenge to encourage consecration to the Blessed Virgin Mary among the young and are, as a result, growing beautifully among young people all over the United States and up into Canada. Their summer camps are held all over North America and are swelling up and bursting with young people eager to honor Mary as their Mother.

Another powerful witness to the fourth commandment is World Youth Day, in which youth from all over the world travel by the millions to go and hear the Holy Father, to celebrate the Mass, to make new friends from everywhere on planet Earth, and to connect with the faith of their fathers and mothers in new, profound, and creative ways. As our culture becomes increasingly severed from its roots, the young long to reconnect with them and draw on the waters of the Tradition. World Youth Day helps that happen and then sends young people back to their own parishes and families to live out the love of God in their day-to-day lives depending on the rich supply of his grace in Christ.

And God supplies this grace via unexpected means. So we see an enormous growth of vocations in the third world, notably Asia and Africa—and we see many of them coming to America and Europe. I well recall talking to an African priest who was visiting the United States as a missionary. He remarked on the history of Christian missions among his people and said that he realized the odd irony of an African now acting as a missionary to America. He said, "In my country, we tell our mothers, 'You carried me when I was young. I will carry you when you are old.'" You could hardly ask for a more beautiful fulfillment of Malachi's prophecy. If you want a simple place to start putting the fourth commandment into practice in your own life, pray that it be fulfilled still more. Then do something small and practical. If you are a mother or father, take some small step to be worthy of the honor paid you by your children. Give them the gift of your time. Tell them you love them. Praise them for something they've done well. Give them a gift, just because. Develop a habit of prayer for them and invite them to join you in your prayers.

Likewise, take some small step to love your own mom and dad today. Give them a phone call. Write them and tell them how grateful you are for all they've done for you. Pay them a visit. If they have already passed on, the wonderful thing about our faith is that "neither death, nor life… will be able to separate us from the love of God in Christ Jesus our Lord" (Romans 8:38–39). So if death has taken them from you, you can still pray for them and ask God to give them his love—and yours.

CHAPTER FIVE

The Fifth Commandment
Against Murder

It's a simple-sounding proposition: "You shall not kill" (Exodus 20:13). Some people, such as pacifists, are absolutists in taking it to mean that all killing is absolutely forbidden. But in fact, that is not what the commandment means.

In Hebrew the fifth commandment forbids—absolutely and without any exception whatsoever—the deliberate taking of *innocent* human life. The inspired author saw no contradiction between the commandment and Israel's numerous wars or the infliction of the death penalty on capital criminals, per Genesis 9:6—"Whoever sheds the blood of man, by man shall his blood be shed; for God made man in his own image." And indeed, this attitude passes down to the Christian tradition as well; thus Paul can say that Caesar "does not bear the sword in vain; he is the servant of God to execute his wrath on the wrongdoer" (Romans 13:4).

The fifth commandment is therefore more accurately rendered, "You shall not murder." That clarification made, it may again be asked whether the proposition "Murder is bad" really required all the smoke and thunder of Sinai. Everybody knows murder is wrong, don't they? So once again it is understandable that some ask why God commands something that everybody already knows and accepts?

Answer: Because as with the command to honor our parents we only know it sporadically, and the same faculty we use for making legitimate distinctions between murder and killing (as in the first paragraph above) can, under the influence of sin, also be used to define murder out of existence when we really, really, *really* want to murder somebody. In short, the commandment exists because situations arise in which we have to be reminded that murder is wrong even when we are strongly tempted to do it.

Murder Made Easy

Our culture is chockablock with examples of this. At the individual level there is, for instance, the "crime of passion." But as our past century attests, oceans of blood can also be spilled by careful non-passionate planners working in clean, well-lit offices in the heart of modernized industrial economies. Modern Americans wonder how the Germans were capable of exterminating eleven million people in their mad zeal for racial hygiene. We congratulate ourselves that we would never fall into such evil. But the reality is that the Nazis gave the same rationales some Americans give for the extermination of roughly five times as many innocent people since 1973. For murder is what *Roe v. Wade* enshrined as the law of the land, just as surely as the Wannsee Conference enshrined it as German policy in 1942. Under the madness of intellects darkened by sin, murder has been declared "necessary" by us, as by the Nazis—in order to maintain security and safety from an "enemy within."

The Germans lied to themselves in redefining the victim so they could exempt themselves from observing the commandment. Jews, Slavs, and Gypsies were reclassified as *untermenschen* [subhumans] or even "bacteria" (it was all very scientifically worded), and their deaths were treated like the death of contagion. Our culture does the same trick: reclassifying babies as "fetal material," sick people as "vegetables," and civilians murdered in unjust warfare as "collateral damage." (For more on the linguistic tricks we play to rationalize evil, see the discussion of the eighth commandment.)

Why do we labor to justify murder? Ultimately there is no rational answer. As C.S. Lewis points out concerning Satan in Milton's

Paradise Lost, when the fallen angel declares "Evil be thou my good," the necessary corollary to that perverse rebellion is "Nonsense be thou my sense."⁹ Sin is contrary to the God who is Truth, so in the final analysis, it makes no sense. In the archetypal case of the Holocaust, somebody might try to find a "reason" for it by saying the Nazis regarded the killing as a matter of self-preservation. They convinced themselves that anything was justified to preserve the *Volk* from their delusional fears of racial impurity. A culture of death is a culture of fear and the Germans whipped themselves into a frenzy of fearful hatred of millions innocent men, women, and children and killed them as enemies of the state and the *Volk*. But in the end, this "reason" makes no sense since the victims did not, in fact, pose any danger. They were innocent civilians—millions of them children—butchered for their ethnicity. The murder was, like all sin, ultimately senseless.

Similarly, our culture has sinfully whipped itself into a frenzy of fear for our comfort. We are enslaved to a spirit that believes anything is justified to preserve ourselves from the burden of raising a "parasite" (as some pro-abortion rhetoric so delicately describes the innocent baby). We could, if we chose, create a sane civilization in which babies are welcomed and adoption is easy; instead we have made a civilization that makes killing the innocent easy and affordable and adoption difficult and expensive. The mad "logic" of the abortion industry follows, covered by further insane lies such as the claim that killing is actually "love." Result: the obscenity of 1.4 million children slain each year for no good reason and a culture that actually boasts about this as a triumph of progress.

As we hone our perverted intellects to defy the utterly clear prohibition against the murder of innocent human life, a kind of Minimum Daily Adult Requirement approach to Catholic moral teaching metastasizes in our souls. We talk as though the goal of life is not maximum love of God and neighbor but minimalist legalism, including a search for loopholes to faith, hope, and charity. Whether the issue on the table is abortion, euthanasia, torture, or unjust war, some way is sought to jigger as many exemptions as possible to the love of God and neighbor. Having enshrined in our culture the notion that comfort, ease, power, and money are more important than innocent human life, we inevitably move on to embrace the proposition that the old, sick, and weak must perish lest they trouble these pursuits. Similarly, the prisoner of war (who is often guilty of nothing more than having been in the wrong place at the wrong time and who the Church says must be treated humanely) is such a threat to us that he is no longer human but an "animal" who can be tortured on the off chance that he might know something.

In all these cases we see the strange absurdity of sin. The weak and old could be cherished and their wisdom borne of suffering learned from, not killed. How much better it would be for the young and strong to create a culture in which they do not have to fear that when they get weak and old, they will themselves be warehoused and murdered. The tortured prisoner could be accorded basic human rights, thereby insuring that *we* need not fear the state should it suspect *us* of wrongdoing. But again we insanely opt for violence as the first option for keeping ourselves "safe"—and succeed only in creating a post-human "civilization" that is increasingly filled with a vigilant fear of our family, our neighbors, and the state.

All this sort of apologetic—whether for abortion, torture, euthanasia, or unjust war—demonstrates the strange itch of fallen *homo sapiens* to find some way to minimize the fifth commandment, just this once, because our particular desire is so intense, or because our particular fear is so desperate and terrifying. Surely the ends will, just this once, justify the gravely sinful means. The wheedling voice says, "What's the *least* I have to do to satisfy God before I can murder for the greater good?"

Can We Ever Justify Murder?

This zeal for death, already in evidence even when there is no justification for taking innocent life, is even more in evidence when we are pretty sure we *do* have justification for taking guilty—or guiltyish—human life. For instance, some would justify the incineration of children in their beds and innocent worshipers at church, simply because these innocent civilians happened to live in Nagasaki during World War II. (Nagasaki's Urakami Cathedral was used by the bombardier to target the atomic bomb.)

Catholic teaching, of course, is very clear: Even in a just war, civilians may *never* be deliberately targeted. Even clearer is the common-sense proposition that, since it is never permissible to deliberately destroy innocent human life: "Every act of war directed to the indiscriminate destruction of whole cities or vast areas with their inhabitants is a crime against God and man, which merits firm and unequivocal condemnation" (*CCC*, 2314, quoting *Gaudium et Spes*, 80).

And yet apologists for the deliberate mass slaughter of civilians at Hiroshima and Nagasaki argue that this particular act of deliberate mass murder directed against innocent civilians was okay and that in this case good ends (a swift surrender) justified gravely evil means. The temptation to ignore the plain meaning of "You shall not murder" knows no borders and, in wartime, it is fatally easy to forget that "The Church and human reason both assert the permanent validity of the *moral law during armed conflict*. 'The mere fact that war has regrettably broken out does not mean that everything becomes licit between the warring parties'" (*CCC*, 2312, quoting *Gaudium et Spes*, 79).

The September 11 attacks demonstrate the ability of fallen man to find rationales for slaughtering innocents on the basis of guilt by association. Civilians working in the World Trade Center were deemed by the terrorists to be part of the economic system of the

United States—and therefore legitimate targets since they were allegedly "collectively responsible" for maintaining the US in fiscal and military health. It would be consoling to tell ourselves that such thinking began with Osama bin Laden, but it is essentially the same thinking that undergirded the terror bombing of civilians in both the Blitz of London by the Nazis and in the terror bombing of Dresden by the Allies. Indeed, a pioneer of such warfare against civilians was General William Tecumseh Sherman in the American Civil War, who adopted exactly the same theory of "collective responsibility" in order to make war on innocent civilians with rape, slaughter, and theft.

These days, the weapons of war for killing innocents have greatly diversified and tend to be more discriminating than nuclear weapons, but the temptation to kill innocents continues and, in some ways, becomes more sinister as the Global War on Terror continues to metastasize. Under President Obama, the U.S. policy of predator drone strikes on targets alleged to be "enemy combatants" has taken on an Orwellian hue. We have "used drones to kill Muslim children and innocent adults by the hundreds. [Obama] has refused to disclose his legal arguments for why he can do this or to justify the attacks in any way. He has even had rescuers and funeral mourners deliberately targeted."[10] How does the U.S. deal with these deaths of innocents, ordered in secrecy, on the basis of the President's will alone, without any due process whatsoever, whether or not the target is an American citizen?[11]

> Mr. Obama embraced a disputed method for counting civilian casualties that did little to box him in. It in effect counts all military-age males in a strike zone as combatants, according to several administration officials, unless there is explicit intelligence posthumously proving them innocent.[12]

The principle at work here is as old as humanity: when we choose to do something gravely evil such as kill innocents, it naturally leads to the search to find ways to justify that choice and to shield ourselves from accountability—such as claiming ex post facto that the dead man had it coming or he wouldn't be dead. (Similar reasoning was deployed by the Sanhedrin when they answered Pilate's request for a legal charge against Jesus by saying, "If this man were not an evildoer, we would not have handed him over" (John 18:30). This is why Just War theory includes not only a *ius ad bellum* requirement (Is there is a just cause to go to war, such as an attack on the World Trade Center?) but a *ius in bello* requirement (Is the war being fought by just means? Are you killing random civilians in the hope you hit a terrorist and then calling the victims terrorists to hide the fact that you are killing civilians?)

What is in evidence here is that, though the letter of the fifth commandment is first and foremost a prohibition against the taking of innocent human life, the spirit of the commandment is that even "good" killing should be avoided wherever possible, and we should go the extra mile to avoid death even when we think we can justify it. In other words, the goal is not Minimum Daily Adult Requirement morality but the maximum love Jesus came to show when he died for the race that butchered him in cold blood. The point of the gospel is to love our enemies, not to search for a threshold where we can kill him without it bothering our conscience. This fact can get lost in our confusing culture-war narratives.

For instance, the Church's teaching on the death penalty seems to create a lot of bafflement. The Church says:

> Assuming that the guilty party's identity and responsibility have been fully determined, the traditional teaching of the Church does not exclude recourse to the death penalty, if this

is the only possible way of effectively defending human lives against the unjust aggressor.

If, however, non-lethal means are sufficient to defend and protect people's safety from the aggressor, authority will limit itself to such means, as these are more in keeping with the concrete conditions of the common good and are more in conformity with the dignity of the human person.

Today, in fact, as a consequence of the possibilities which the state has for effectively preventing crime, by rendering one who has committed an offense incapable of doing harm—without definitively taking away from him the possibility of redeeming himself—the cases in which the execution of the offender is an absolute necessity "are very rare, if not practically nonexistent." (*CCC*, 2267, quoting John Paul II, *Evangelium Vitae*, 56)

Seems straightforward. But whenever this teaching gets mentioned in millennial Catholic America, two basic sorts of people come out of the woodwork to argue with each other—and with the Church.

Arguing the Death Penalty

The first sort is the one who assumes that the death penalty, war, euthanasia, and abortion are morally equivalent issues. Mention the death penalty, and these folks show up faster than you can say "pro-life hypocrite," a favorite term of theirs to denounce people who oppose abortion but favor the death penalty or support a given war. And to be sure, if one favors an *unjust* war or an *unjust* application of capital punishment while still claiming to be pro-life, then the epithet is accurate. But one who favors *just* war or the *legitimate* application of the death penalty while always opposing abortion and euthanasia is no more *ipso facto* a hypocrite than a surgeon who cuts into living flesh to save a patient is the moral equivalent of Jack the Ripper.

The deliberate taking of innocent human life can never be justified. The deliberate taking of life in self-defense or in defense of society *can* sometimes be justified. The two different forms of killing simply are not morally equivalent.

Pope John Paul II was as pro-life as they come. But he never declared that the death penalty was a crime "no human law can legitimize," as he clearly defined abortion and euthanasia to be.[13] That's because he had read Romans 13 and knew that in a just application of the death penalty, the person being killed has it coming, and his or her death is justly meted out by the state to protect innocent people from being harmed.

Having cleared that elementary point out of the way, we then hear from the second sort of person, whom I call the *death penalty maximalist*. This person dissents from magisterial teaching in this: While the Church seeks to *limit* the death penalty as much as possible, the death penalty maximalist seeks to execute as many as possible. Such a person often strongly suggests that the Church's push to limit or abolish the death penalty is immoral, heretical, and should be treated with contempt.

The maximalist does not deem the *Catechism* wrong merely in saying that "the cases in which the execution of the offender is an absolute necessity are very rare, if not practically nonexistent" (which is a fallible practical judgment based on things like prison safety and technology). No, the maximalist sees the *Catechism* as wrong *in principle*: The death penalty is not merely to protect the community but to (allegedly) serve justice! And since it is a matter of principle (allegedly), then it follows that we *must* execute as many capital criminals as possible so that Justice may be served as completely as possible. For the maximalist the onus is on the Church to show why a capital criminal should be spared, not on Caesar to show why he should be killed. And so, among Catholic maximalists a variety of arguments are put forward to argue that this development of the Church's teaching is, in fact, erroneous.

Some cite sundry theological authorities pre-dating the development of the Tradition in order to show that the Magisterium has no right to opinions earlier theologians do not share (St. Thomas's approval of the death penalty often gets cited here, on the assumption that Thomas somehow trumps *Evangelium Vitae*). Such arguments ignore the fact that Thomas—and any other faithful theologian— would be horrified at being pitted against the magisterial teaching of the Church. They also overlook the very salient point that theologians are not infallible.

Some quote Scripture (especially Genesis 9:6) and oppose it to *Evangelium Vitae*, declaring that Pope John Paul II's "personal opinions" do not equal magisterial teaching, even if they are in an encyclical. Some even go so far as to denounce death penalty minimalists or abolitionists such as Pope Benedict XVI,[14] not merely as Catholics who are making a different prudential judgment, but as heretics, cowards, weaklings, moral posturers, heartless fiends who mock the suffering of victims, etc.

Some make strange *non sequitur* claims that "Opposition to the death penalty is really just an attempt to divert our attention from abortion" or "Not that many people get executed and although sometimes innocent people are executed it's a statistically insignificant number." (Try telling *that* to the innocent man about to be hanged.)

Bottom line: For the dedicated death penalty maximalist, if you aren't in favor of maximum death for the maximum number of criminals, you are a Bad Catholic, even if you are the Pope and all the bishops of the world. To quote one maximalist in the blogosphere who warmly applauded the death of the penitent murderer Teresa Lewis[15] and rebuked those who were not eager to slay her:

In more balanced ages, men did not so easily arrogate to themselves the right to spare murderers, et al. They knew, both as Christians and as members of true cultures, that such reprobates were to be offered the assistance and gifts of the Church, and then to be sent out of this world forthwith, to seek mercy from God. It is, I often think, an insidious side effect of the creeping disease of Modernism (which is far from defeated) that some of us Catholics fear death so much that we dare not trust even the likes of this Teresa scoundrel to it.[16]

The notion that Christian piety is best demonstrated by "trusting" somebody else to death is a curious one, echoed with alarming frequency in the conservative Catholic blogosphere. Here, for instance, is an amazing argument I received from a reader of my blog:

Don't any of you self-righteous death penalty opponents ever read the Bible? As he was hanging on the cross, Jesus promised Paradise to the felon who confessed the justice of the death penalty. (See Luke 23:39–43)

The strange conflation of dogmatic death penalty maximalism with the core Catholic doctrine of Christ's saving grace is a classic illustration of how a human tradition can get fuddled with Sacred Tradition. For of course, the actual biblical teaching is that Jesus promises paradise *to the one who places his faith in him*, not to those who place their faith in the American penal system. Indeed, Jesus himself, presented with an open-and-shut case of capital guilt under the Law of Moses—a woman taken in the very act of adultery—did not inflict the death penalty. Instead he, like the Church that followed him, chose mercy (see John 8:3–11).

If we are to hold to a fundamentalist take on the death penalty, then we need to be consistent. The good thief, who says, "We are receiving the due reward of our deeds" (Luke 23:41) regards not merely capital punishment but *crucifixion* as just. Do those who assert "salvation by faith in the death penalty" therefore assert that *crucifixion* is a just form of capital punishment? If not, why not? If so, then when do they plan to lobby to institute crucifixion in these United States? And what about all the other capital crimes in Scripture besides murder? Do maximalists propose we follow Iran and Saudi Arabia and put homosexuals, adulterers, cross dressers, and sassy teenagers to death? We don't hear much about the need for witch burning or stoning idolators, blasphemers, and atheists to death. Yet all these offenses against the Ten Commandments were, at one time, as subject to the death penalty as murder. Yet, death penalty maximalists almost never go there—except the clearly demented ones.

The reason they don't is simple: the Church is right. Mercy is preferable to mercilessness and our culture suffers from a major case of bad conscience, which demonstrates that maximalists are haunted by this fact every day. That is why even most maximalists do not want to really be so maximal as all that.

Some might call that hypocrisy. I call it the recognition that this is not ancient Israel and that the leaven of mercy in the Church leavens culture as well. I also call it a sort of residual prudence with the sense to know that urging the power to kill undesirables on a rapidly de-Christianizing and increasingly barbarous culture of death is rather like sending a delegation of ancient Christians to Nero to demand that he crack down on all those weird new religions infesting the empire. We Christians may get a lot more than we bargained for.

In the end, all the maximalist can really say is that the death penalty is not dogmatically defined by the Church as intrinsically immoral. True. Neither is playing in traffic. It's still an idea whose time has passed, and the Church urges us to oppose it.

In fact, the Church is perfectly sensible to affirm that Caesar has the theoretical right to wield the sword in some cases—and yet urge him to do so as rarely as possible. Why? For the same reason we would defend a doctor's right to perform an amputation on our child's injured leg if necessary—while also begging him to make such surgery an absolute last resort after all else has been tried to save her. After all, God has made it clear that he prefers mercy and takes no "pleasure in the death of the wicked" (Ezekiel 18:23; see Matthew 9:13). So while Romans 13 places the sword in the hand of Caesar to execute judgment on capital criminals or to make just war under certain circumstances, so Scripture also clearly shows us instances when criminals guilty of capital crimes (for example, the adulterous murderer King David) have been spared and other remedies for desperate sin employed.

In short, despite the fundamentalist readings of Genesis 9:6 by death penalty maximalists, the Catholic tradition has *always* regarded the death penalty with flexibility and has lots of precedent for urging that it be applied as sparingly as possible. When God himself has not inflicted the death penalty with rigidity, neither need we. Paul, who was an accessory to the lynch murder of a completely innocent man (see Acts 7:58; 8:1), was *not* given his just desserts as a blasphemer and a violent man; rather he was shown such great mercy that he became an apostle of Christ. Mercy is preferable to death wherever possible.

This development of magisterial teaching, seen in *Evangelium Vitae* and reflected in the *Catechism*—and development it is, not Pope John Paul II's dismissible personal opinion—means that the Church's basic posture is that the onus is on Caesar to show that execution is necessary, not on the human person to show why his dignity makes him worthy of not being killed.

The point is that the dignity of the human person derives not from his works, whether good or ill, but from the God who made him in his image and likeness. The Church does not deny that Caesar, for the sake of the common good and the defense of the innocent, *may* execute a capital criminal. But the Church urges that if the common good is not threatened by a criminal behind bars, then mercy rather than strict vengeance is the better course. And in the First World, especially here in the United States, the practical result is that Catholics should work for the abolition of the death penalty.

This seems reasonable to me, and I am therefore, following the magisterium, a death penalty minimalist. That is, while I do not concede that the death penalty is the moral equivalent of abortion or euthanasia, I think its application should be restricted to absolute necessity. Indeed, this seems *a fortiori* reasonable with a penitent brother or sister, who not only is no longer a threat to others but also seeks to serve Christ. I think the best course is for them to serve a life sentence rather than be put to death. That's the minimalist position in a nutshell.

Aiming Higher

As we wrestle with these various attempts to minimize even so obvious a commandment as "You shall not murder," we see afresh the truth about the Ten Commandments, and most especially this commandment: They are given in order to reinforce minimal moral requirements in the face of our fallen race's assaults on reason. They show us not the heights of sanctity but the bottommost limits of morality. "I have not slaughtered my neighbor" is not exactly a glittering example of the splendor and holiness of Christ's love. But for us fallen humans, it's a start. The fear of the terrible judgment that awaits the impenitent murderer is, among other things, what the author of Proverbs has in mind when he says, "The fear of the LORD is the beginning of wisdom" (Proverbs 9:10).

That wisdom, if we let it grow in our souls, points us to a painful diagnosis: We need a Savior. Indeed, the Savior himself warns us that the commandment against murder is not satisfied merely because we haven't actually shot the guy who cut us off on the freeway. As Jesus points out in the Sermon on the Mount:

> You have heard that it was said to the men of old, "You shall not kill; and whoever kills shall be liable to judgment." But I say to you that every one who is angry with his brother shall be liable to judgment; whoever insults his brother shall be liable to the council, and whoever says, "You fool!" shall be liable to the hell of fire. (Matthew 5:21–22)

In short, if you hate somebody from the heart, you are already guilty of murder, because the heart is where murder is born. The bad news, of course, is that all of us can attest to the fact that our hearts are little murder hatcheries where the serpent's eggs of a thousand resentments can sit quietly incubating if we do nothing to smash them. The good news is that Jesus stands ready at a moment's notice to give us the grace and power of his Holy Spirit to not only begin healing us of our anger over past hurts, but to make us able to overcome those hurts and even bless and love our enemies. So powerful is his grace to accomplish this that countless saints have even gone to their death praising God in song and seeking the forgiveness and eternal happiness of even their murderers, just as their Lord did.

Of course, most of us will not be tested to that extreme. But all of us need to learn the charity that makes such love a reality—and we can. The trick, as ever, is to start small, beginning with the acknowledgment that we do, in fact, need Jesus' help to love. Some of us have bigger struggles than others, but all of us require the help of the Spirit. Small steps can take us a very long way.

So, as George MacDonald says, "He who will not let us out until we have paid the uttermost farthing, rejoices over the offer of the first golden grain in payment. Easy to please is he—hard indeed to satisfy."[17] We cannot pat ourselves on the back as having arrived at sanctity merely because we keep a tight lid on our anger and don't actually throttle our neighbor to death when he has the loud party. On the other hand, under the power of grace, even the smallest effort to love and forgive is a starting place in those desperate moments when we are really tempted to murder the jerk. And since God is pleased with our faltering efforts as much as with the great deeds of giants like St. Paul, he can turn the widow's mite of our struggles with anger into a great spiritual fortune for his glory.

CHAPTER SIX

The Sixth Commandment
Against Adultery

Our culture pretty much winks at adultery these days, sort of the way Maurice Chevalier lecherously ogles "girls, girls, girls" in some old musical number. Adultery is sold as a charming but lovable fault, as with that adorable rascal Bill Clinton. Or else it is sold as exciting and sexy, as with Brangelina.

Citing "You shall not commit adultery" in our culture is bad form among the wine-and-cheese crowd, like belching in church—if such clever and trendy people went to church. Vast swaths of our culture rush to reply to such embarrassing displays of crude moralism with scarcely a movement of the gray matter. "Judge not"! (Matthew 7:1), they shout from the commanding heights of culture and media.

This most popular of biblical verses, trotted out to excuse every sin under the sun, has double the impact on Christians familiar with John 8. It was, after all, an adulterous woman our Lord defended against the mob.

> The scribes and the Pharisees brought a woman who had been caught in adultery, and placing her in their midst they said to him, "Teacher, this woman has been caught in the act of adultery. Now in the law Moses commanded us to stone such. What do you say about her?" This they said to test him, that they might have some charge to bring against him. Jesus bent down and wrote with his finger on the ground. And as they continued to ask him, he stood up and said to them, "Let him who is without sin among you be the first to throw

a stone at her." And once more he bent down and wrote with his finger on the ground. But when they heard it, they went away, one by one, beginning with the eldest, and Jesus was left alone with the woman standing before him. Jesus looked up and said to her, "Woman, where are they? Has no one condemned you?" She said, "No one, Lord." And Jesus said, "Neither do I condemn you; go, and do not sin again." (John 8:3–11)

And so huge numbers of biblically illiterate people who are apostles for sexual license repeat the only verse they know—"Judge not"—while huge numbers of biblically literate Christians feel guilty and have no clue what to do about adultery. Any suggestion that adultery is evil and a grave sin is seen by both believers and secularists alike as reprehensibly Pharisaic. We all act as though the only real sin is the pruny frown of disapproval leveled at a heart that, in the words of Woody Allen, "wants what it wants."[18]

Cultural Conditioning

Contemporary secular culture prides itself on having "outgrown" sin and the need for mercy. That is because post-modernity is, hands down, the most sexually deranged culture in the history of the world. Rome, in its final stages of decadence, nonetheless confined that decadence to its upper classes. We have achieved the unprecedented marvel of making sexual depravity a broadly middle-class phenomenon—and feeling really good about ourselves in the process.

Such feats are not achieved in a day. They take long periods of conditioning and progressive steps of "pushing the envelope." Back in the thirties and forties, the manufacturers of culture loved making movies about "gay divorcees." As a general rule, the divorced couple would get back together at the end of the movie. But the idea was still instilled in a broad audience of would-be sophisticates that divorce was rather a cheery thing than otherwise, undertaken by witty adults like Cary Grant and Katherine Hepburn, who bantered cleverly and understood that the breakup of a marriage was mostly an occasion for brilliantly scripted repartee.

As time went on and the culture of divorce began to permeate the membrane of the movie screen and work its way into pop culture, we saw an increasingly warm acceptance of philandering and *Seven Year Itch* thinking until, in the disastrous decade of the seventies, we put a bullet to the brain of the family by approving the catastrophe of no-fault divorce. We have gone on to encourage every unstable person who watches a piece of dreck like *Eat, Pray, Love* to ditch his or her family and "do what I need to do for me" in their unending quest for personal fulfillment through the latest trophy wife or boy toy.

Indeed, we have turned adultery into an industry. Whole businesses are devoted to helping facilitate adulterous "flings," as they are called. And the press coverage of such enterprises is of the puff-piece variety, full of the frisson of "Ooh! How naughty!" For instance:

> "Life is short. Have an affair."
>
> That's the slogan of the Ashley Madison dating service, a website for people who want to cheat on their partners. That's right, unlike traditional Internet dating sites—where you're expected to say you're unattached no matter what the truth is—Ashley Madison is honest about its duplicity. Unlike *match.com*, with its married interlopers, Ashley Madison isn't about to break the hearts of innocent singles who only want to live happily ever after with someone who loves Elvis Costello as much as they do. And although its mission can be perceived as very wrong (for the record: cheating is bad!), the fact that it claims 3.2 million members suggests that it's also doing something right.

For starters, the commercials are hilarious. One television spot shows a glamorous couple in the throes of passion. A title card reads, "This couple is married...but not to each other." In another ad, a man retreats to the sofa to escape his obese, snoring wife while a voice-over declares, "Most of us can recover from a one-night stand with the wrong woman, but not when it's every night for the rest of our lives."[19]

All this has been assisted, of course, by the advent of the Pill, by the tendency of the media to trot out the word *taboo* every time some fresh depravity is being contemplated by the envelope pushers, and by our own addiction to the sins of the flesh. After all, how can you condemn the next perversion without risking the possibility that somebody will condemn you for embracing the last one?

Now, it is certainly the case that there are invalid "marriages" between people who had no business attempting marriage. Our culture has, among other things, distinguished itself from all previous human societies by inventing the concept of the teenager (unknown till about sixty years ago). It is a useful marketing demographic by which the servile consumer state has managed to create about two and a half generations of people who are encouraged to embrace all that is worst about both childhood and adulthood and prolong themselves in this state for as long as possible. As a result, we Boomers of Generation Narcissus managed to inculcate in ourselves and our children a fatal formula of childish irresponsibility combined with a raging sense of entitlement to adult sexual perks that has had disastrous consequences for the family such as a 50 percent breakup rate. Given such radical immaturity, it is easy to understand the major spike in invalid marriages and subsequent annulments we have witnessed in the past forty years.

But the fact remains that there is also real adultery taking place as well: that is, real betrayal of real vows made by people who knew what they were doing on their wedding day. And that whole trail of tears begins in the heart with real sinful choices. The moment we commit ourselves to the proposition that our happiness can only be found through selfishness and betrayal is the moment that all bets are off for any sane sexual ethic. The gospel of Judas is the enemy of the gospel of Jesus.

Indeed, the sexual revolution of the sixties and seventies was a tremendous boon for traitors and Judases. Adultery was euphemized using perky, upbeat words like "affair" and "fling," while the manufacturers of culture tended to downplay the whole "stab in the back, knife to the heart, shredding of children's lives" aspect of it. But that is the heartless heart of adultery and it requires grace and healing for both the victims and the perpetrator who has made his or her own body an accomplice to the lie that we can put asunder what God has joined.

A Matter of Forgiveness

As Pope John Paul II pointed out, we speak with our bodies as well as our tongues.[20] The highest pledge of fidelity and love we can make to another person is the sexual act. When we make that pledge we speak, with our bodies, a promise of total self-giving to the other. When we break that pledge by adultery, we commit one of the greatest betrayals one human being can commit against another. It is a lacerating act of cruelty aimed at the heart of the family, at children, and at all human trust, with repercussions that are felt for generations and across all layers of society.

That is why Jesus *forgave* the woman caught in adultery. You don't forgive people who are not guilty; you excuse them. The woman caught in adultery was guilty as sin, taken in the very act. She was hauled out of the sack—covered in the shame of what she had done—and brought before Jesus. When she looked him in the eye (if she could bear to), she had enough sense not to say, "The heart wants what it wants," nor to chirp, "Life is short. Have an affair," nor to burble, "Don't judge." Instead she felt the reproaches heaped upon her, insincere as the mob was. She knew that, however much she was being used by them as a pawn in a game to destroy Jesus, somewhere there was a heartbroken wife or her own cuckolded husband. She knew the betrayal she had committed against a family.

Jesus knew it too—and forgave her. When he spoke to her he did not say, "Yours was a beautiful love misunderstood by harsh and judgmental prigs." He said, "Go and sin no more."

Adultery, like all other sins, can be and is forgiven by Christ every day. The deep bleeding wounds and scars it leaves behind can be healed by the power of Christ's mercy. But mercy is for *sinners*. And adultery remains what it has always been: a grave and cruel betrayal. If we do not see this—if we fill our minds with rubbish about how the children will be "resilient" and the new girlfriend or boy toy will help us self-actualize better—we will not receive mercy because we will not admit that we need it. We will not be like the penitent woman or like Jesus. Rather, we will be like the mob with stones who were convinced that they were sinless and qualified to judge themselves and others.

A sense of shame for the sin of adultery is the necessary prerequisite for the forgiveness of the sin. Let us pray that we recover that sense of sin, so that we may know the grace not just of forgiveness but of never sinning again. Generations yet unborn will thank us for it.

CHAPTER SEVEN

The Seventh Commandment
Against Theft

"You shall not steal," says Exodus 20:15. Once again the Decalogue presents us with an injunction that seems like common sense but is also fraught with all sorts of difficulties and distinctions.

Consider, for instance, the fact that a Catholic writer like me has the obligation to never write an original thought in my life. Indeed, one of the few earthly perks of being a Catholic writer is that I get to steal somebody else's great ideas all the time and call it "being faithful to the Tradition." The Catholic faith consists of a huge body of ideas that I did not invent and can neither add to nor subtract from. It is common, not esoteric. My task as a Catholic writer is to dip into this body of common revelation and ladle it out for people to contemplate. That's not theft; that's fidelity.

This problem of distinguishing between what is common to all and what is specifically mine or yours is the puzzle that lies behind the commandment against stealing. If another Catholic writer were to write an essay on the seventh commandment, he could go on for thousands of words and even thousands of volumes and never trespass against the seventh commandment. But if he were to write:

> "You shall not steal," says Exodus 20:15. Once again the Decalogue presents us with an injunction that seems like common sense but is also fraught with all sorts of difficulties…

and continue on without mentioning that I wrote this first, that's the particular species of theft known as plagiarism.

Certain things are rightly and properly ours. That is the positive truth that the negative prohibition against stealing undergirds. We demonstrate this knowledge of natural law (before we can read or write and often before we can form complex sentences) when our little brother swipes our cookie, and we hit him on the head with our plate and take the cookie back. We also learn it from our own slapped hands if we take something we shouldn't. Natural law tends to be learned via natural consequences. Fairly quickly we discover concepts like "rights," including the reality that you don't have the right to my stuff and I don't have the right to yours.

To be sure, some leftists have attempted to describe all property as "theft," just as some libertarians have, with equal folly, attempted to describe all interest in the common good as "socialism" or "communism." But we must not, as C.S. Lewis reminds us, listen to the over-wise or the over-foolish giants. "Opposite evils, far from balancing, aggravate each other."[21] The Tradition warns against both envy (the besetting sin of the poor) and greed (the besetting sin of the rich) and directs us to keep our balance by recognizing what is properly ours and what is common.

Pride, Envy, and Deceit

One obstacle to applying the seventh commandment justly is the fact that it is often tempting to simply assume that one's own tribe is all that matters. White settlers who would never have considered claim-jumping on other white settlers had no problem stealing land from Native Americans. That wasn't *stealing*; that was *Manifest Destiny*. Only when Native Americans started to count as fellow human beings did white Americans begin to think of the theft of their land as, you know, *theft*.

Similarly, for many people one twenty-dollar bill stolen from a stranger on the bus is theft, but music on the Internet is free for the taking. Indeed, for some people "sharing" music has somehow become a positive right. And the justification for that right is that the musicians being robbed "have enough money already."

This brings us to one of the odd engines of theft in the human psyche: envy. The notion that fuels the sin of envy is that harming somebody else is tantamount to justice. Unlike with jealousy, envy does not seek to better itself by keeping up with the Joneses but to take the Joneses down a peg so that they are no better than us. It is the characteristic sin of a democratic culture as distinct from pride, the characteristic sin of an aristocracy.

Our envy-driven culture can be seen even in the strange way people compete, not to be fraudulent winners, but to be fraudulent losers. Envy gives rise to fake Holocaust memoirs and cock-and-bull stories such as *A Million Little Pieces*.[22] In ages past women pretended to be Anastasia, the heir to the throne of all the Russias, and gained fame dazzling people with fake pretensions of royalty. Now they write *I, Rigoberta Menchú* and gain fame with fake pretensions of victimhood.[23]

This is not to say the Tradition sides with the rich against the poor. On the contrary, one of the remarkable things about the Church is how empathetic she is with the poor. As the *Catechism of the Catholic Church* says concerning the duty of those with more than they need:

> St. John Chrysostom vigorously recalls this: "Not to enable the poor to share in our goods is to steal from them and deprive them of life. The goods we possess are not ours, but theirs." "The demands of justice must be satisfied first of all; that which is already due in justice is not to be offered as a gift of charity":
>
> When we attend to the needs of those in want, we give them what is theirs, not ours. More than performing works

of mercy, we are paying a debt of justice. (*CCC*, 2446, quoting St. John Chrysostom, *Hom. In Lazaro*, 2, 5: PG 48, 992; *Apostolicam Actuositatem*, 8, 5; St. Gregory the Great, *Regula Pastalis*, 3, 21: PL 77, 87)

So there is a reason Robin Hood is a legend who emerges from the Catholic tradition. Indeed, by Catholic reckoning Jean Valjean, the hero of *Les Misérables*, never *stole* a loaf of bread; he took what was rightfully his to feed his family. The Catholic tradition is notably sympathetic to Lazarus and notably rough on the rich man who was oblivious to him (see Luke 16:19–31), warning that much will be required of those to whom much is given (see Luke 12:48). The man who hoards goods he does not need while his neighbor goes without basic necessities is, in Catholic reckoning, the real thief.

But the Church is also acutely aware of the fact that just because you are a victim doesn't mean you can't be a sinner too. The poor man who steals MP3s off the Internet or the lazy young man living a hand to mouth existence by snatching old ladies' purses for change is not acting on some noble principle of helping the poor. He's just stealing because he's too much of a slob to pay for what he's stealing.

Taking and Giving

The commandment against stealing is one of the areas where the Christian tradition requires us to think proportionally. Stealing a CD is not the same as knocking over a 7-11 or robbing a Brinks armored car. Yet it should also be noted that stealing can be the occasion of grave interior sin, even when the thing stolen is quite trivial. St. Augustine, it will be recalled, had his first experience of his capacity for sin in stealing a few pears as a kid. It's the sort of incident that would not even be noticed by the sheriff of Dogpatch—just some boys being naughty. But Augustine discerned in it his first encounter with, and dark delight in, radical evil.[24]

I suspect that's because theft is the most accessible of the grave sins mentioned in the commandments. Most of us will never murder anybody, and adultery requires a certain state in life. But any idiot can steal, and any idiot often does. It's one of the things we can't not know is wrong, but it's the easiest grave sin to commit.

Some people want to overlook small acts of theft and focus on things like corporate greed. Conversely, on the principle that a billion dollars is a statistic but fifty bucks can be understood, others want to focus their ire on the small-time thief and the welfare queen while ignoring the massive raiding of the public coffers by corporate fat cats. The general rule of thumb is that, while justice is blind, we should probably take most care to oppose the thief for whom we feel the most empathy (especially the thief who may be looking back at us in the mirror). So, for instance, the votary of capitalism could do with more concern about the corporations that irresponsibly urged people to take out disastrous subprime loans ("Free toaster! Come and get it!"), while the leftist could stand to remember that nobody held a gun to the heads of the irresponsible people who took out the loans—and that those people were often strongly motivated by the desire to get something for nothing.

The flip side of all this business of theft, of course, is generosity. "It is," says our Lord, "more blessed to give than to receive" (Acts 20:35). The way to avoid the sin of stealing is to cultivate not the habit of "not stealing" (there is no such animal, just as there is no such thing as the habit of not smoking) but the habit of *giving*. Scripture says, "God loves a cheerful giver" (2 Corinthians 9:7). So Paul counsels, "Let the thief no longer steal, but rather let him labor, doing honest work with his hands, so that he may be able to give to those in need" (Ephesians 4:28).

Mind you, I speak here not as a saint but as that Catholic writer with the task of ladling out the Tradition, including parts that I neither enjoy nor obey with notable distinction. I hope in the Lord Jesus to one day be that "cheerful giver," but I am more of a greedy grabber. So until I am a saint, I continue to lamely give as I can and do my duty of reporting what the Tradition says until I believe it enough to live it. Let us pray for one another that even thieves might discover the generosity of Christ in us.

St. Dismas, the good thief, and St. Nicholas, patron of thieves, pray for us.

CHAPTER EIGHT

The Eighth Commandment
Against Bearing False Witness

It is a curious fact that the same book of Exodus that informs us of the command "You shall not bear false witness against your neighbor" (Exodus 20:16) begins with the story of a good solid lie:

> Then the king of Egypt said to the Hebrew midwives, one of whom was named Shiphrah and the other Puah, "When you serve as midwife to the Hebrew women, and see them upon the birthstool, if it is a son, you shall kill him; but if it is a daughter, she shall live." But the midwives feared God, and did not do as the king of Egypt commanded them, but let the male children live. So the king of Egypt called the midwives, and said to them, "Why have you done this, and let the male children live?" The midwives said to Pharaoh, "Because the Hebrew women are not like the Egyptian women; for they are vigorous and are delivered before the midwife comes to them." (Exodus 1:15–19)

Some readers of this text are understandably troubled about this bald-faced lie. Others might argue that it proves the immorality of the Old Testament. Others see in it an act of divine approval for lying for a good cause. The confusion only grows as the inspired writer cheerily continues:

> So God dealt well with the midwives; and the people multiplied and grew very strong. And because the midwives feared God he gave them families. (Exodus 1:20–21)

The biblical author confronts us with a paradox: On the one hand he records a command against bearing false witness, which will, again and again throughout the biblical tradition, be reiterated: Avoid lies because the devil is a liar and the father of lies (see John 8:44). Tell the truth because God is the God of truth. Scripture bangs away at this repeatedly:

> There are six things which the LORD hates,
>   seven which are an abomination to him:
> haughty eyes, a lying tongue,
>   and hands that shed innocent blood,
> a heart that devises wicked plans,
>   feet that make haste to run to evil,
> a false witness who breathes out lies,
>   and a man who sows discord among brothers. (Proverbs 6:16–19)

> Truthful lips endure for ever,
>   but a lying tongue is but for a moment.
> Deceit is in the heart of those who devise evil,
>   but those who plan good have joy.
>
> …
>
> Lying lips are an abomination to the LORD,
>   but those who act faithfully are his delight. (Proverbs 12:19–20, 22)

> God…never lies. (Titus 1:2)

> If we say we have fellowship with him while we walk in darkness, we lie and do not live according to the truth; but if we walk in the light, as he is in the light, we have fellowship with one another, and the blood of Jesus his Son cleanses us from all sin. (1 John 1:6–7)

At the same time, as the story of the midwives attests, the inspired authors realize that sometimes telling the truth, the whole truth, and nothing but the truth can get innocent people killed.

> And the men said to [Rahab], "Our life for yours! If you do not tell this business of ours, then we will deal kindly and faithfully with you when the LORD gives us the land." (Joshua 2:14)

> My son, be attentive to my wisdom,
>   incline your ear to my understanding;
> that you may keep discretion,
>   and your lips may guard knowledge. (Proverbs 5:1–2)

> Do not give dogs what is holy; and do not throw your pearls before swine, lest they trample them under foot and turn to attack you. (Matthew 7:6)

What Scripture does not do—and later Christian theology will be tasked with doing—is tell us how to reconcile these two realities of life. As we puzzle over this, let's go back to some basic facts.

The Truth of the Matter

Truthful speech is the currency of a happy and virtuous human community. The *Catechism* gets right to the point:

> "A *lie* consists in speaking a falsehood with the intention of deceiving." The Lord denounces lying as the work of the devil: "You are of your father the devil,…there is no truth in him. When he lies, he speaks according to his own nature, for he is a liar and the father of lies." (*CCC*, 2482, quoting St. Augustine, *De mendacio* 4, 5:PL 40:491, John 8:44)

> Lying is the most direct offense against the truth. To lie is to speak or act against the truth in order to lead someone into

error. By injuring man's relation to truth and to his neighbor, a lie offends against the fundamental relation of man and of his word to the Lord. (*CCC*, 2483)

The *gravity of a lie* is measured against the nature of the truth it deforms, the circumstances, the intentions of the one who lies, and the harm suffered by its victims. If a lie in itself only constitutes a venial sin, it becomes mortal when it does grave injury to the virtues of justice and charity. (*CCC*, 2484)

By its very nature, lying is to be condemned. It is a profanation of speech, whereas the purpose of speech is to communicate known truth to others. The deliberate intention of leading a neighbor into error by saying things contrary to the truth constitutes a failure in justice and charity. The culpability is greater when the intention of deceiving entails the risk of deadly consequences for those who are led astray. (*CCC*, 2485)

Since it violates the virtue of truthfulness, a lie does real violence to another. It affects his ability to know, which is a condition of every judgment and decision. It contains the seed of discord and all consequent evils. Lying is destructive of society; it undermines trust among men and tears apart the fabric of social relationships. (*CCC*, 2486)

If truthful speech is demanded of the merely secular social order, even more is this true of the Church. For in the end, all the Church has to offer is faith, and faith requires trust that the gospel is true and not a fraud perpetrated by liars. A civilization built on lies is doomed, but a Church that lies is damned.

And yet, as with stealing, murder and adultery, there are times when we all want to bend the truth, nuance it, shade it, or outright lie about something, as the Hebrew midwives did. When the Nazis come to the door asking if you are hiding any Jews, you don't take them to the hideout in the attic out of a slavish commitment to absolute transparency.

Nonetheless, the commandment stands, precisely because it is fatally easy to tell ourselves that because our extremely special good end justifies it, we can go ahead and lie and it will be okay. We can even tell ourselves that our lying is noble and beautiful and good and start comparing ourselves to the Hebrew midwives who (we feel sure) were commended by God for lying.

The problem is, that's not so, according to a vast array of Catholic teachers from Augustine to Aquinas to the present. Indeed, St. Thomas summarizes the Catholic tradition when he states that *every* lie is a sin, without any exception whatsoever. How then does he deal with the Hebrew midwives? He writes:

> The midwives were rewarded, not for their lie, but for their fear of God, and for their good-will, which later led them to tell a lie. Hence it is expressly stated (Exodus 2:21): "And because the midwives feared God, He built them houses." But the subsequent lie was not meritorious.[25]

In short, they were right to want to save lives, but wrong to save lives by lying. This is a surprise for many modern Christians, who have absorbed from pop culture the notion that lying "in a good cause" is fine. For instance, there was a recent kerfuffle when members of a pro-life organization went into some Planned Parenthood clinics, lied about their identities and purpose, and did what they called a "sting operation." Pretending to be sex traffickers seeking abortions, they covertly filmed themselves being interviewed by Planned Parenthood workers and then released the video with the claim that it exposed that organization's support for prostitution. Many supporters of the prolife movement regarded this as a great coup. Planned Parenthood shot back that the video was heavily edited, that the clinic workers were humoring the clients while trying to figure out how to contact the authorities, and so on. Soon the whole thing devolved into a "he said, she said" dispute, and the nine-day wonder was over, leaving us with two facts.

The first fact is that a great many Christians were completely ready to embrace what the pro-life organization had done as morally legitimate and to denounce anybody who questioned these tactics. The Internet was abuzz with people saying things like, "Criticizing this brave act constitutes support for killing babies!"

No. It doesn't. It constitutes support for the age-old Christian condemnation of lying and the equally age-old Christian insistence that good ends do not justify evil means (see Romans 3:8).

This illustrates the second fact revealed by that controversy: that the Church's teaching is there not because we millennial Catholics live in special times that our naïve ancestors could not have imagined, facing challenges they never dreamed of, but because the temptation to lie is as old as the hills.

See if this scenario sounds familiar. There is a growing movement whose dangerous error is insinuating itself into society and gravely endangering many innocent people. Fear and anger spread as decent Catholic folk find that God doesn't seem to be answering their prayers to quell the menace. Finally somebody says, "We need to take radical action and infiltrate the group in order to expose what they are doing. We are AT WAR! And precious souls are at risk if we don't take radical action NOW! I'm not going to stand around quibbling about a few little lies while innocents are facing a horrible fate!"

That was the situation—in the fourth century, when the Priscillianist heretics were endangering not bodies but souls and leading them (as Catholics believed) to the everlasting fires of hell. As the heresy grew and Catholics became desperate, somebody proposed lying about their identity and purpose in order to infiltrate the group, expose the false teaching, and save souls from the terrifying doom of the second death (see Revelation 20:11–15). This is when St. Augustine wrote his book *Against Lying,* in which he denounced exactly this course of action and argued strenuously that lying for Jesus is *lying* and is therefore a sin, no matter how noble our goal may be. Indeed, lying is a sin "by its very nature," as the *Catechism* (see *CCC,* 2485) makes extremely clear and the Tradition has always said.

Nothing New

Some in the pro-life movement will reply to the parallel between lies to Priscillianists and the pro-life group's lies to Planned Parenthood, "Do you equate this forgotten theological quarrel with abortion? We're talking about life and death!" The incredulity contemporary pro-life culture feels at comparing saving bodies from death with saving souls from heresy marks one of the essential differences between modernity and antiquity: the conviction that the death of the body is far more serious than the death of the soul. Augustine and his flock took it for granted that the second death was a far worse thing to fear than the first death. They believed Jesus when he said, "Do not fear those who kill the body but cannot kill the soul; rather fear him who can destroy both soul and body in hell" (Matthew 10:28). So Augustine felt keenly (as his flock did) the danger posed by false teaching and the urgent desire to protect people from it. It was as real a temptation for his flock to lie to the Priscillianists as it is for a modern pro-life advocate to lie to Planned Parenthood. Yet Augustine, faced with the same temptation as we are, looks across the ages at us with a cool head and says, "You cannot lie for Jesus. You cannot do it to save bodies, and you cannot do it to save souls."

Some will reply that Augustine lived in a simpler time before the rise of Nazism, and giant organizations like Planned Parenthood required us to take desperate measures. Untrue. Yes, St. Augustine and St. Thomas lived before Nazis and Planned Parenthood, but they did not live before evil people harmed innocents, because they did not live before Cain and Abel. So when St. Thomas answered in the affirmative the question of whether lying is always a sin, he also considered—and refuted—the objection that lying is virtuous in desperate situations:

> Objection 4. Further, one ought to choose the lesser evil in order to avoid the greater: even so a physician cuts off a limb, lest the whole body perish. Yet less harm is done by raising a false opinion in a person's mind, than by someone slaying or being slain. Therefore a man may lawfully lie, to save another from committing murder, or another from being killed.[26]
>
> Reply to Objection 4. A lie is sinful not only because it injures one's neighbor, but also on account of its inordinateness, as stated above in this Article. Now it is not allowed to make use of anything inordinate in order to ward off injury or defects from another: as neither is it lawful to steal in order to give an alms, except perhaps in a case of necessity when all things are common. Therefore it is not lawful to tell a lie in order to deliver another from any danger whatever. Nevertheless it is lawful to hide the truth prudently, by keeping it back, as Augustine says (*Contra Mend.* x).[27]

Jesus illustrates just this principle when, in respect for the grave sinner's freedom, he allows the evildoer to make his stubborn choices after all attempts to warn him and call him to repentance are exhausted. He warns Judas again and again ("One of you is a devil/One of you will betray me/What you are going to do, do quickly" [John 6:70; 13:21, 27]) and, in the end, Jesus lets Judas "outwit" and "defeat" him at the cost of his own life. Yet Jesus never tells a lie and never tempts Judas to commit a sin.

At this point, the defender of the pro-life "sting operation" is likely to say, with some impatience, "Are you seriously suggesting that telling a white lie to Planned Parenthood—for the purpose of saving lives, mind you—is as serious a sin as deliberately killing an unborn child?"

No. Neither does St. Thomas, who, after making clear that every lie is a sin, also makes clear that every lie is not a mortal sin.[28] Like all sane people, he recognizes that sticking scissors in a baby's brain dwarfs the comparatively venial sin of lying.

But he also recognizes that a venial sin, even one committed for a good end (as sins usually are) does not become a virtue by comparison to a bigger sin. This is, in fact, exactly why the Church makes the distinction between mortal and venial sin and adopts neither the folly of saying all sin is the same nor the folly of saying venial sin is okay.

So if I am, say, an impulsive teenager from a poor family who swipes ten bucks from an open cash register to pay for a Christmas present for my sick grandmother, I have committed a venial sin of theft. If I swipe that ten bucks from the pocket of a corporate crook sauntering down Wall Street who just stole one billion dollars from some hapless investors, I am *still* sinning—even if my victim is a far worse sinner. Worse, if I begin to congratulate myself that my lunch hour predations on corrupt Wall Street banksters are actually virtuous since their sins are so much worse, I am not growing in virtue, but hardening myself in sin.

The danger of our tendency to let the mortal sins of others drown out the sinfulness of our own venial sins and even turn them into imagined virtues is simply this: in the Church's tradition venial sins are gateway drugs to more serious sins. And the perfect way in which to allow the addiction to take hold is to tell oneself that not only is the venial sin not a sin, it is a positive virtue.

This is seen in the radical contrast between Jesus' absolute refusal to lie or tempt even Judas to do evil versus the sting operation's treatment of the Planned Parenthood worker. Whatever the noble long-range goal of the sting was, the actual effect was not merely that lies were told, but that they were told for the purpose of deliberately tempting the worker to commit the mortal sin of making herself an accessory to murder by helping arrange an abortion.

Some will argue that since she worked for Planned Parenthood she "would have done it anyway with somebody else who really was pregnant." But we do not, in fact, know that. There are documented cases of Planned Parenthood workers who have been greatly troubled about their work and who have abandoned it with the encouragement of pro-life witnesses, just as many alcoholics have been greatly troubled by their alcoholism and turned away from it by the grace of God and with the help of disciples of Jesus. Using lies to tempt a Planned Parenthood worker into making herself an accessory to murder so that we can expose Planned Parenthood is like offering a bottle of whiskey to an alcoholic and saying, "What the heck. He's a drunk anyway. So what it if destroys him? It'll really expose how the alcohol industry ruins lives!" In other words, the great overlooked danger of lying—even for a good cause—is the corruption it engenders in the liar and damage it does to the one to whom we lie.

The Choice for Truth

So we confront a stark choice. We can say, "OK, lying *is* always a sin" (albeit often a venial one), and proceed to form our thoughts and actions in light of the Church's teaching on that point. We can decide that we will refuse to lie, even in a good cause, refuse to try to justify even venial lying, and find other ways to deal with the challenge of living in a world where not everybody is owed the complete truth. For instance, we can realize that the real trick with the Nazis at the door is not to lie well but to hide your Jews well. Then you can invite the

Nazis in (and they will come in whether you invite them or not) and offer them tea as they search. You are under no obligation to volunteer the fact that the Jews are hidden behind the false wall in the attic.

> The *right to the communication* of the truth is not unconditional. Everyone must conform his life to the Gospel precept of fraternal love. This requires us in concrete situations to judge whether or not it is appropriate to reveal the truth to someone who asks for it. (*CCC*, 2488)

A society that maintains discretion is a very different thing from a society that is built on lies, even lies for Jesus. We can face this fact and refuse to tell lies, even in a good cause. If we do that, we will find freedom, according to Jesus (see John 8:32).

What's Another Word for Euphemism?

Or we can say, as someone said to me, "If lying is always wrong, then what that pro-life group did was not lying." That is, we can continue the attempt to justify lying by *calling it something else*. Start doing that drug, and we find only more and more slavery, for the deliberate choice to lie inevitably shackles us to the deliberate choice to lie about our habit of lying. This demonstrates the particularly corrosive way in which the embrace of lying always leads to the destruction of truthfulness and even sanity. And this is most clearly seen by our culture's embrace of the widespread use of euphemism.

Euphemism is the practice of replacing old and short English words like "lies," "murder," and "war" with longer terms like "augmented verbal accuracy strategies," "termination of human assets," and "limited kinetic operation." The idea is to make the ugly thing smell nicer by perfuming it with something that sounds softer, or scientific, or otherwise more palatable. George Orwell once said, "Political language—and with variations this is true of all political parties, from Conservatives to Anarchists—is designed to make lies sound truthful and murder respectable, and to give an appearance of solidity to pure wind."[29] In the endeavor to sell us lies, the Father of Lies loves euphemism perhaps more than any other tool—because the other word for "euphemism" is "lie."

So, for instance, the ante-bellum South spoke of slavery as "our peculiar institution." Likewise, the U.S. government recently replaced the old and plain word *torture* with the much nicer and more scientific sounding *enhanced interrogation*. Funnily enough, the Gestapo did exactly the same thing, renaming their torture techniques *Verschärfte Vernehmung* or "sharpened/enhanced interrogation."

Speaking of the Gestapo, totalitarian states are masters in the art of euphemism. For instance, the mass murder of European Jewry was given the pleasant and efficient title of a "final solution." Similarly, the Communists liked to speak of "liquidating" rather than killing political opponents. In the East, Chinese Communists had a charming way of supplying euphemistic titles for the mass murder of citizens, such as "the Great Leap Forward" or "Cultural Revolution."

Of course, today terms like "final solution" inspire exactly the horror that the more plainspoken "mass murder of millions of innocent Jews" used to inspire. Likewise, when we speak of the government "liquidating a high-value target," we all know that this means "killing a human being." *Euthanasia*—which was concocted to cover up the unpleasant fact that a doctor was murdering a patient—now simply means "a doctor murdering a patient," so new euphemisms like *death with dignity* are put forward. And the term *abortion*, which was originally intended to give a gleaming, clinical cover for child slaughter, now simply means "child slaughter." That's why pro-abortion zealots don't like to be called "pro-abortion" but now demand to be called "pro-choice." And *abortion* is now called *reproductive care intervention*.

Thus goes the euphemism treadmill. A euphemism is a thin piece of perfumed paper wrapped around the stinking corpse of an evil act. The problem is, the corpse's stench overwhelms the scent as the bloodiness of the deed soaks through the paper. So a new euphemism is required to cover over the old, bloody paper. Thus, while a phrase like *limited kinetic operation* might for a while be the new hotness in euphemisms for war (and, as of this writing, the United States is currently engaged in over seventy-five *limited kinetic operations*), it is only a matter of time before *limited kinetic operation* will simply mean war and a new euphemism will be required. No matter how many ways and times you tell a lie, it's still a lie. And it all starts, typically, with the gateway drug of venial lies.

As in Augustine's day, so now: lies corrupt, and in the final diabolical irony, lies don't work. They are invariably Faustian bargains that take our soul and give us *nothing* in return. The good thing we hope to gain by cutting corners turns to ashes, and we are left with only the devil's laughter ringing in our ears.

So after the thrill of watching Planned Parenthood briefly embarrassed, what did the pro-life movement get from the sting operation? Corruption and loss. While Christians were busy concocting rationales to incorporate approval for lying into their moral calculations, Planned Parenthood sent out fundraising pleas to the pro-abortion faithful, announcing that pro-lifers are, by their own admission, liars and declaring the videos they made "heavily edited"—with a predictably outraged and generous responses from their donor base. Result: Christians radically harm their witness to the God of truth first by lying and then by trying to defend lying; Planned Parenthood gets richer and more powerful. It's a lesson we could learn from a dozen *Twilight Zone* episodes if we will not learn it from the Church.

"For Fellowship"

Of course, not all or even most temptations to lie involve lies to or about perceived enemies in desperate arenas of moral combat. After all, how many Nazis do you meet these days? Far more often, we are tempted to lie to or on behalf of family and friends. It is notable that the eighth commandment focuses not on lies in the abstract but on *bearing false witness against your neighbor.* In an ancient Semitic culture, the complex ties of tribe and family—as well as the sharply defined class relationships of rich and poor, royal and common, man and woman, kinsman and alien—provided ample temptations for suck-uppery, extortion, false witness, and oppression of the weak.

This commandment constitutes one of the Lord's bedrock defenses of the weak and marginalized, for whom he, again and again, declares himself the Avenger (see Deuteronomy 10:18 and Jeremiah 49:11, for example). The one who tells lies in order to oppress and exploit these disenfranchised people stands in particular danger of the divine wrath.

That said, we flatter ourselves to the point of absurdity if we think we are any less in danger of grave evil than a bunch of shepherds living in the ancient Near East. It is the wife who asks, "Does this dress make me look fat?" or the friend with the awful toupee who asks, "Well? What do you think?" or the boss who writes the paycheck who occasion many of our strongest temptations to lie. There is something about face-to-face contact with another human being that tends to create bonds, in both the good and the bad sense of that word. When we get to know somebody at all, we find that we pad our speech so as to cushion the truth, in order to guard their feelings. Often this is a perfectly legitimate thing to do. But it can also tempt us not merely to be diplomatic but to refuse to face hard realities, such as the alcoholic husband, the addicted child, or the philandering friend.

The tendency to assume the best of people we have come to know is normal and healthy as far as it goes. It's the lubricant that makes social relationships possible. But when we let it slide into denial, or sycophantic flattery, or outright lying in order to protect ourselves or those we care about, then we head into places where it becomes all too easy to bear false witness.

An example of this tendency—and the way to resist it—can be seen in Robert Bolt's play *A Man for All Seasons*, when the Duke of Norfolk tries to persuade Thomas More to sign the Act of Succession repudiating the pope and making King Henry VIII head of the Church in England:

> Norfolk: Oh, confound all this.... I'm not a scholar, as Master Cromwell never tires of pointing out, and frankly I don't know whether the marriage was lawful or not. But damn it, Thomas, look at those names.... You know those men! Can't you do what I did, and come with us, for fellowship?
> More: And when we stand before God, and you are sent to Paradise for doing according to your conscience, and I am damned for not doing according to mine, will you come with me, for fellowship?[30]

A contemporary example of this tendency to allow tribal ties to lead us to lie is the disaster of the priest abuse scandal. People seldom get up in the morning saying, "Today I will bear false witness against my neighbor just for the heck of it." Instead they start by giving extra weight to what Fr. Beloved Priest says, because, well, after all, we *know* Fr. Beloved Priest. He's one of *us*. Meanwhile, the angry mom and the kid with the shocking claim are *them*. Indeed, often the bitter words of outrage and denunciation from a victim of Fr. Beloved's betrayal only make it easier to shuffle mom and the kid off to the "them" category.

"Hey!" we say, "They could be *anybody*. Fr. Beloved has a long and distinguished career! He baptized my daughter and tells funny jokes and dried my tears when my mother died." And it would be very convenient if his accuser *were* just anybody: some riffraff or gold digger off the streets. We don't want to hear it. It's got to be tinfoil-hat talk.

So we shade the truth, first of all to ourselves, and downplay the complaint. And as the complaints against Fr. Beloved pile up from other sources, we have to keep adding to the investment of faith we have in Fr. Beloved, even as we begin to put extra effort into attacking his accusers. Before we know it, we have whole groups of people laboring to protect the reputation of Fr. Beloved and laboring to destroy the reputation of his accusers. All this seems to work swimmingly—right up until the DNA samples show conclusively that Fr. Beloved indeed has a daughter, or the child porn is found on his computer. At which point everybody starts asking themselves how they could have been so blind.

The answer is both simple and hard: "You ignored the commandment against bearing false witness. You gave preference to somebody you know and like over somebody you don't know who threatened you with the truth." It is this tendency to favor members of one's own tribe over the outsider that the Law of Moses has in view when it warns Israel:

> For the LORD your God is God of gods and Lord of lords, the great, the mighty, and the terrible God, who is not partial and takes no bribe. He executes justice for the fatherless and the widow, and loves the sojourner, giving him food and clothing. Love the sojourner therefore; for you were sojourners in the land of Egypt. (Deuteronomy 10:17–19)

T.S. Eliot once said that humankind cannot bear very much reality. Certainly this is the witness of Scripture and of history. Tell the truth and you may be vindicated like the hero of *Meet John Doe* or *Mr. Smith Goes to Washington*. But odds are equally good you might get thrown down a well like Jeremiah, shot to death like Dr. Martin

Luther King, Jr., or crucified like Jesus. It is partly because truth is so scary that God reminds us of the gravity of betraying it.

When we lie or bear false witness, the bad currency of speech drives out the good, and the sin and the judgment are the same thing. A society that accepts false witness and lying language into the core of its way of thinking is a society that is teaching itself to lose touch with reality. The United States discovered this in the 1860s, when all the piled-up lies about black men and women as "property" became insupportable, and reality came roaring back with a vengeance. The same principle is now at work as we experience the fruit of our habit of self-delusion with abortion and other crimes of the culture of death.

For a lying spirit tends to float. It refuses to stay where we want it to (such as defending only the lies of the sexual revolution and leaving the rest of our wits unclouded). Instead, a lying spirit causes us to pursue folly in every sphere of life. The culture that can delude itself that the newborn baby gasping out its last breath on the table is just a "born-alive fetus" or a "blob of tissue" is a culture that can convince itself that the way to prosperity and happiness is to go into massive and unpayable debt. The radical folly behind the economic meltdown of 2007 is that it was and remains the product of a culture that denies reality.

In short, "God is not mocked" (Galatians 6:7). As with all sins against natural law, the punishment is simply the natural consequence of our wicked and stupid choices. The way to avoid these consequences is as simple as it is challenging: Don't make the wicked and stupid choice to lie. Rather, as Paul says, "Therefore, putting away falsehood, let everyone speak the truth with his neighbor, for we are members one of another" (Ephesians 4:25). And the way to do that is to ask for the grace of God in Christ to overcome the temptation to bear false witness against your neighbor and, far more, to cultivate a habit of speaking the truth in love.

Jesus' promise is plain: "You will know the truth, and the truth will make you free" (John 8:32). Not least among the blessed fruits of that simple yet powerful act of Christian discipleship is just being able to sleep better at night. As Mark Twain noted, "If you tell the truth you don't have to remember anything."[31]

CHAPTER NINE

The Ninth Commandment
Against Coveting Your Neighbor's Spouse

As we come to the ninth commandment, we again are in disputed territory. As you will recall from the discussion of the first commandment, the Ten Commandments have been split up in different ways: Some Protestants break apart the first commandment (yielding what I call the 1.5 commandment against graven images). The Catholic tradition, in contrast, leaves the first commandment whole and breaks apart the following text:

> You shall not covet your neighbor's house; you shall not covet your neighbor's wife, or his manservant, or his maidservant, or his ox, or his donkey, or anything that is your neighbor's. (Exodus 20:17)

The breakage is summed up this way:

> Ninth commandment: You shall not covet your neighbor's wife.
> Tenth commandment: You shall not covet your neighbor's goods.

We will bracket the discussion of the commandment against coveting your neighbor's stuff till the next chapter except to note one point: Moderns should pay attention to the fact that the Tradition shows, in a place we would hardly expect it, a curiously feminist streak. Whereas the code delivered to Bronze Age men simply tumbled the wife in with all the other property, the Catholic catechetical tradition pulled her out of the inventory and makes a rather sharp distinction between having your eye on the neighbor's Prius and having your eye on his missus. And of course this goes for coveting the neighbor's husband too.

Before we can talk about coveting the neighbor's spouse, we need to talk about coveting. The striking thing about the ninth and tenth commandments is that they are absolutely unenforceable by any human agency in the world—except for ourselves. For covetousness is a sin we commit in our *souls*, not in our bodies.

To be sure, we can covet our neighbor's spouse and bed him or her, but then we are committing adultery, for which there is already a whole 'nother commandment. Likewise, we can covet our neighbor's goods so much that we stick a .38 in his ribs and demand his wallet. But that's called stealing, and the seventh commandment has that one covered. Coveting, on the other hand—just sitting and stewing over someone's hot wife, sweet ride, or good looks—happens in the holy of holies called the human soul and is knowable ultimately only by us and God.

This brings us back to the fact that the Ten Commandments are deeply rooted in the language of covenant with God, not in mere civics. The lesson of the ninth and tenth commandments against coveting is the same as that of the Sermon on the Mount:

> You have heard that it was said, "You shall not commit adultery." But I say to you that every one who looks at a woman lustfully has already committed adultery with her in his heart. (Matthew 5:27–28)

In short, sin is rooted in the heart. What we do with our bodies is merely the fruit of the evil that comes from the heart. So the real work of curing sin has to begin there too.

It is worth noting that it was the law against covetousness that was Paul's undoing. He had the external observance thing down pat. But when it came to honestly assessing what was in his heart in the glaring light of the Law, he was dismayed:

> What then shall we say? That the law is sin? By no means! Yet, if it had not been for the law, I should not have known sin. I should not have known what it is to covet if the law had not said, "You shall not covet." But sin, finding opportunity in the commandment, wrought in me all kinds of covetousness. Apart from the law sin lies dead. I was once alive apart from the law, but when the commandment came, sin revived and I died; the very commandment which promised life proved to be death to me. For sin, finding opportunity in the commandment, deceived me and by it killed me. So the law is holy, and the commandment is holy and just and good. (Romans 7:7–12)

Paul's enormous insight about the Law came from this experience, seen in the light of Christ. For Paul, the Law is good as an X-ray machine is good. It is indispensable for the healing process, revealing the cancerous tumors of the soul that would otherwise remain hidden and metastasize. But the Law cannot heal us. It looks within and tells us what's wrong with us—and that's *all*. It cannot help us get better any more than repeated x-rays will heal the tumor. They that are sick need the Physician that Paul had encountered on the Damascus road and in the sacramental and liturgical life of the Church.

When we discussed the sin of adultery, we talked about the sort of romantic sentimental rubbish our culture throws at us to justify it. Some variation on, "It's sad to belong to someone else when the right one comes along," or, "If loving you is wrong, I don't wanna be right," or, "How can it be wrong when it feels so right?" is typical for us cinema-besotted fools when we are trying to convince ourselves to break the sixth commandment. Popular culture tends to associate the sin of adultery with the courage of the rebel against a cruel world, not with the sin of lust.

There's a sort of diabolical intuition behind that, since rebellion is the characteristic act of the devil and pride is his characteristic sin. So it is often the case that one can likewise covet the spouse of another not out of lust but out of pride, just as we covet someone's car or job. We can set our sights on defeating the competition, seeing their spouse as a trophy to be gained and exulted over. Not a few people in this world regard sexual relations as a competitive sport and the other human beings involved as either the opposing team or the ball to be moved down the field. Such people have not even the comparatively sympathetic scent of the romance-besotted adolescent. Rather they exude the stench of mere *conquest*.

Very often such people, having won the prize and humiliated the competition, throw the trophy wife or boy toy away and begin again on somebody else's spouse. Their true love is themselves. For such people, others are simply apparatuses to be used in obtaining the thrill of victory. Such people do indeed covet their neighbor's spouse in exactly the same way they covet their neighbor's house or goods.

That is why the prescription of the Catholic tradition for defeating covetousness of your neighbor's spouse is, when you think about it, deeply insightful. It is not cold showers, or self-flagellation, or all the other elaborate tricks for distraction.

It is modesty.

Consider that word. It is a word that addresses not only the sin of lust, but the sin of pride as well. To be modest is not merely to forego dressing like one of the cast of *Jersey Shore*. It is also to be humble. It is to be so at peace and content in one's own skin that we do not feel the craving to impress somebody else, nor to induce lust in the hearts of strangers, nor to walk off with the trophy babe or the beefcake hunk

in order to show those clowns back in high school that we've gradu-
ated to sexual maturity. Modesty short-circuits the sin of covetousness *and* the sin of pride by teaching us contentment, happiness, and
peace with the boundaries God has placed in our lives. It is lived and
cultivated by deliberate choices we make in thought, word, dress, and
action, with the help of grace. It is a quiet yet enormously powerful
virtue that begins, as all wisdom does, with the fear of the Lord, but
which reaches its fruition not from the Law, but from grace—the
grace which springs from the purity of heart Jesus speaks of in the
sixth Beatitude.

The good thing about modesty, as with all virtuous habits, is that
we can begin to cultivate it immediately if only the will to do so is
there.

Not that will is enough by itself. As Paul attests, our hearts are a
war zone:

> We know that the law is spiritual; but I am carnal, sold under
> sin. I do not understand my own actions. For I do not do
> what I want, but I do the very thing I hate. Now if I do
> what I do not want, I agree that the law is good. So then it
> is no longer I that do it, but sin which dwells within me. For
> I know that nothing good dwells within me, that is, in my
> flesh. I can will what is right, but I cannot do it. For I do not
> do the good I want, but the evil I do not want is what I do.
> Now if I do what I do not want, it is no longer I that do it,
> but sin which dwells within me.
>
> So I find it to be a law that when I want to do right, evil lies
> close at hand. For I delight in the law of God, in my inmost
> self, but I see in my members another law at war with the law
> of my mind and making me captive to the law of sin which
> dwells in my members. Wretched man that I am! Who will
> deliver me from this body of death? (Romans 7:14–25)

If even the great St. Paul could not look at his soul under the X-ray of the Law without finding covetousness there, then odds are good you and I will not be able to either. Welcome to the human race! The moral of that discovery is not that you must grit your teeth and try harder to be sinless. Paul tried that and it didn't work. The moral, rather, is to realize what Paul did after that great cry of helpless need:

> Thanks be to God through Jesus Christ our Lord! So then, I of myself serve the law of God with my mind, but with my flesh I serve the law of sin.
>
> There is therefore now no condemnation for those who are in Christ Jesus. For the law of the Spirit of life in Christ Jesus has set me free from the law of sin and death. For God has done what the law, weakened by the flesh, could not do: sending his own Son in the likeness of sinful flesh and for sin, he condemned sin in the flesh, in order that the just requirement of the law might be fulfilled in us, who walk not according to the flesh but according to the Spirit. For those who live according to the flesh set their minds on the things of the flesh, but those who live according to the Spirit set their minds on the things of the Spirit. To set the mind on the flesh is death, but to set the mind on the Spirit is life and peace. For the mind that is set on the flesh is hostile to God; it does not submit to God's law, indeed it cannot; and those who are in the flesh cannot please God.
>
> But you are not in the flesh, you are in the Spirit, if the Spirit of God really dwells in you. Any one who does not have the Spirit of Christ does not belong to him. But if Christ is in you, although your bodies are dead because of sin, your spirits are alive because of righteousness. If the Spirit of him who raised Jesus from the dead dwells in you,

he who raised Christ Jesus from the dead will give life to your mortal bodies also through his Spirit who dwells in you.

So then, brethren, we are debtors, not to the flesh, to live according to the flesh—for if you live according to the flesh you will die, but if by the Spirit you put to death the deeds of the body you will live. For all who are led by the Spirit of God are sons of God. (Romans 7:25—8:14)

In short, we begin not by trying harder, but by placing ourselves in the presence of God, asking for forgiveness for our sins and asking for the grace to obey him now—and then trying to live that out by some simple and humble act of love for God and neighbor. Light (and conquest of covetousness) will come step by step. Rather than covet the neighbor's spouse, we will seek their genuine happiness, which is to be found in growing in love for his or her own family, not by being seduced away from them by our selfish desires. And this will eventually lead us to confront not just our disordered sexual appetites, but all our disordered desires—bringing them into harmony with the will of Jesus.

It is to all those other disordered desires that we now turn as we look at the last commandment.

CHAPTER TEN

The Tenth Commandment
Against Coveting Your Neighbor's Goods

As we noted in the previous chapter, the Catholic tradition of cate-chesis has tended to break up Exodus 20:17 into two command-ments. The ninth commandment bids us not to covet our neighbor's spouse. The focus of the tenth commandment is on coveting his stuff.

> You shall not covet your neighbor's house; you shall not covet…his manservant, or his maidservant, or his ox, or his donkey, or anything that is your neighbor's.

As we also saw, the law against coveting is directed not against an action but against a sin of the heart. Just as the sin of adultery begins with the sin of coveting your neighbor's spouse, so the sin of theft is born when you covet your neighbor's stuff.

That said, it should also be noted that not just theft can spring from the sin of covetousness, it is possible to covet more than simply your neighbor's stuff. You can also covet his very life. For example, out of four assassinated presidents, only one was killed by prideful vainglory. John Wilkes Booth did not want for fame, talent, wealth or women and did not shoot Lincoln out of envy. He saw himself as the Avenger of the South, Brutus to Lincoln's Caesar. But the other three assassins were emphatically small men who just wanted to take down somebody powerful in a spasm of envious vengeance. From James Garfield's killer Charles Guiteau (a "disappointed office seeker") to Leon Czolgosz (his confession: "I didn't believe one man should have so much service and another man should have none") to the failure Lee Harvey Oswald, we are looking at small men rankling with covetousness over the success of their victims. Covetousness can be the birthplace not only of theft but of murder.

Covetousness is typically the sin of the poor and the weak, just as greed is typically the sin of the rich and the powerful. This is one of hell's strategies. The devil always sends temptations into the world in pairs in the hope that in running from one kind of sin, we will run straight into the arms of its opposite. The poor man Czolgosz congratulates himself for his valor in siding with the working class as he guns down the rich man McKinley in cold blood. While Scrooge congratulates himself on his hard work and thrift, he grinds Bob Cratchit and sends Tiny Tim to an early grave.

In a world filled with tremendous greed and the celebration of wealth—often amassed by wicked people using unscrupulous means—it becomes extremely easy to justify covetousness. But covetousness is perhaps the most fruitless form of sin there is. With greed you at least experience possession (though not real enjoyment) of the thing you own. With lust you at least get sexual pleasure now and then, though not love. With gluttony you get the taste of food, though not the satisfaction. But with covetousness you get no compensation at all. A jealous man can at least use his jealousy to go out, work hard, and get the same car his neighbor has. But an envious man sits there doing nothing, waits till it is night, and then slashes the tires on his neighbor's car instead of lifting a finger to accomplish any good at all. Jealousy can be redeemed. Envy, the green-eyed daughter of covetousness, must simply be killed.

Envy is a beast that only gets hungrier when you feed it. Give it its head, and covetousness imprisons you in a cycle of bitterness. Covetousness is rooted not in the thing you think you want but in your refusal to accept from God the peace that he desires to give you in your circumstances—whatever they may be. Covetousness piles sin on top of poverty.

St. Francis, following his Master, found a different way: the way of Lady Poverty, which celebrated his dependence on God with freedom and joy. She's as possible to embrace today as in Francis' day.

We have the choice to rely on God to give meaning and value to life. It's again the choice to think of the Christian life not merely as fulfilling the Minimum Daily Adult Requirement of "not sinning" but of aiming for the heavens with the maximum amount of faith, hope, and charity the Holy Spirit can give us. In short, the recognition of our souls as the real battleground in the war for holiness inevitably draws us to look beyond the shadow of virtue, the Ten Commandments, to the fulfillment of virtue, which is a life empowered by the Spirit to live the Beatitudes.

PART TWO
The Beatitudes

Seeing the crowds, he went up on the mountain, and when he sat down his disciples came to him. And he opened his mouth and taught them, saying:

"Blessed are the poor in spirit, for theirs is the kingdom of heaven.

"Blessed are those who mourn, for they shall be comforted.

"Blessed are the meek, for they shall inherit the earth.

"Blessed are those who hunger and thirst for righteousness, for they shall be satisfied.

"Blessed are the merciful, for they shall obtain mercy.

"Blessed are the pure in heart, for they shall see God.

"Blessed are the peacemakers, for they shall be called sons of God.

"Blessed are those who are persecuted for righteousness' sake, for theirs is the kingdom of heaven.

"Blessed are you when men revile you and persecute you and utter all kinds of evil against you falsely on my account. Rejoice and be glad, for your reward is great in heaven, for so men persecuted the prophets who were before you." (Matthew 5:1–12)

CHAPTER 11

Blessed Are the Poor in Spirit

The gospel calls us to a paradox in its teaching on poverty. In telling us that the kingdom of heaven belongs to the poor in spirit, it bids us, among other things, to recognize in the face of the poor the face of Christ. Secular culture is resistant to this idea. We like to hurriedly emphasize the words *in spirit*, in order to avoid looking into the faces of the hobos, winos, toothless geezers, street kids with fleas, addicts, schizophrenics, brawling illiterates, and smelly people who are, after all, what the word *poor* often refers to.

To be sure (as we shall see in a moment) poverty of spirit is a good thing. But Luke's record of this beatitude is simply "Blessed are you poor"—period (Luke 6:20). Because of this, Catholic Tradition has preserved what is known as the "preferential option for the poor": the assumption that the poor, being among the most defenseless in our midst, not only require the care of the rest of society and not our contempt but are "blessed": that is, somehow *set apart and above* the rest of us by God, simply by virtue of the fact that they are poor. There's no clause in there about their being virtuous, deserving, like-able, mentally stable, or hygienic. The blessing is an act of pure grace and generosity on God's part.

We should linger over that fact for a while and not hurry *too* quickly to spiritualize the saying, still less to tell the poor to get with the program and pull themselves up by their bootstraps. To be sure, self-improvement is a fine thing, and there's nothing wrong with helping people improve their economic fortunes. But our Calvinistic culture is overly quick to assume that the poor are the way they are because they are shiftless, and so on. Our first impulse is to blame. The gospel does not take this route.

That's why Christ's first words to the poor are words of blessing, not of criticism or advice. He does this despite the fact that the Jewish tradition from which he springs—for example, in the book of Proverbs—is chockablock with all sorts of blame and advice for the poor, just as Christian culture is.

> A little sleep, a little slumber,
>> a little folding of the hands to rest,
> and poverty will come upon you like a vagabond,
>> and want like an armed man. (Proverbs 6:10–11)

> A rich man's wealth is his strong city;
>> the poverty of the poor is their ruin. (Proverbs 10:15)

> Poverty and disgrace come to him who ignores instruction,
>> but he who heeds reproof is honored. (Proverbs 13:18)

The gospel has something deeper to say: namely, that Christ, who was rich, became poor for our sake, and so he identifies himself in a peculiar way with the poor and calls us to see himself in them (see Matthew 25:31–46; 2 Corinthians 8:9). Our task, first, is to *see that*: to hold our tongues from the reams of blame and advice we itch to give the poor and to contemplate the reality that in encountering them, we are encountering Jesus Christ.

At the same time, the gospel has no truck with the romantic leftist notion that the poor are automatically noble by virtue of their poverty. In other words, they are blessed, but they are not automatically saints. Suffering *can* sanctify, but it need not necessarily do so. As we ourselves know when we suffer, it is not the case that mere suffering automatically makes us disposed to hear and obey the Holy Spirit. Part of the fundamental human dignity of the poor is that they retain the human power to choose beatitude or damnation.

And so, for instance, a hundred years ago, a poor man whom Christ blessed along with all the poor roamed the streets of Vienna, struggling to keep food in his belly, living among the rat-infested underclass. His father had beaten him when he was a child, and his beloved mother had died of cancer. He dreamed of being an artist and spent years in poverty as he strove to achieve his vision. But for all that, Adolf Hitler was not transformed into a saint.

That is the paradox of this beatitude. When *looking* at the poor, we must see the face of Christ, who identifies himself with them. But we must not make the easy assumption that the poor identify themselves with Christ.

This is particularly true when we face our own poverty. We may know for certain that our humble Lord is "God with us" in all the desert places of our life, but we dare not suppose that merely being poor is a guarantee of our sanctity. We must recognize our poverty—whether financial, emotional, spiritual, or physical—as a great opportunity but not presume from it that we are therefore paragons of virtue. The immense and tragic blunder of communism was that it transformed sympathy for the poor into the assumption of their sanctity and used that cocksureness as a justification for a kind of secular theology of envy that claimed the right to murder of millions in class warfare.

Here then is the twofold promise of this beatitude: You can spot a poor man easily, but you will never see his spirit. That's why we are not to judge but are simply to assume that the poor we meet are Jesus and act accordingly. It is only our own poverty that we can transform, that we might be truly poor *in spirit*. If we see Christ in the faces of the poor and treat them as we would treat him, we shall be blessed. If we acknowledge our poverty and need of God and look to him to fill our need, we shall be twice blessed.

CHAPTER TWELVE

Blessed Are Those Who Mourn

I remember it like it was yesterday. The kitchen phone was ringing insistently on the other side of the wall as I awoke. I had gone to bed exhausted with sorrow and fear the night before, having returned from the hospital where my dad lay snoring loudly in the depths of a coma. Just as my eyes opened, I heard Mom pick up the phone and say, "Yes?" I held my breath and could hear the stroke of my pulse in my ears. Then I heard my mom moan, "Ohhhhhhhhh!"—as though all the sadness of the earth was in it.

My heart pounded, and I jumped out of bed, numbly groping for the door. The worst thing in the world had finally come. I rushed to my mom and held her for a minute, then went down the hall to tell my older brother that Dad was dead. Trembling, I went back to my bedroom, fell to my knees, and bawled, asking God to take Dad's soul and grant him peace. I still feel the grief as I write about it, twenty-nine years later.

When I tell people this story, they often tear up even if they know neither me nor my dad. That tells us something hugely important about what a truly personal experience is.

Our culture, intensely individualistic as it is, tends to identify *personal* experience with *esoteric* experience—something only knowable to a select few individuals, not commonly shared, and incommunicable to the non-initiate. When people say, for instance, that religious belief is personal, they often mean that it is supposed to be private and not public because it is supposedly esoteric. Therefore, it's supposed to be one of those things we don't include in polite conversation.

Now, to be sure, there is something properly private about the intensely personal experience of mourning. We aren't supposed to intrude on somebody's grief with platitudes and "buck up" speeches. But it is emphatically not true that mourning is therefore something esoteric, only knowable to a select few individuals, not commonly shared, and incommunicable to the non-initiate. On the contrary, mourning is universal and common—as are all our deepest experiences. In fact, the things that are most universal are also the things that are the most personal. Everybody falls in love. Everybody feels fear. Everybody has known delight. Everybody wonders what the point of life is.

And everybody mourns. We may think that when we mourn we are utterly alone. But the truth is that we join the ranks of all the weeping children of Adam and Eve and feel in our marrow what the great pagan poet Virgil called "the tears of things."[32]

We experience this in mourning not only the death of loved ones but also the loss of things, places, times, abilities, hopes, dreams, and many of the other goods of this passing world. We can feel it in the passing of a pet. The ache comes upon us when we go back to that Little League field of our summer youth, now rank with weeds and slated to have a condo built on it next month.

Grief assails us as we think of the things we never got to say before someone died. We find ourselves nursing a drink in the wee hours, wishing we'd screwed up the courage to pick up the phone and tell Grampa how much we loved him, before Alzheimer's took away his ability to know who we were. We see that dream of going to France slipping irrevocably away. We face the verdict of the doctor bravely, but in our hearts there is sorrow for our own plight and for the beloved whom we will leave helpless on the shore of this world as the bark of death carries us away, with us powerless to stop it.

Mourning stalks us. We know that sooner or later our time will come, and we hope to ward it off. So we chase death and loss away as much as possible. We often act out of a sort of superstitious fear that it is "catching," so we avoid those in mourning lest we get some of it on us should they erupt in some unseemly display of shouts or tears or begging for the past to return. But for all that, mourning comes to us anyway—because God wills that we be blessed.

The blessing, says Jesus, comes not in the form of avoidance of mourning but in the form of comfort. The great model and prophet of this truth—Isaiah—spoke to the Jewish people in the midst of their great national trauma, the Babylonian Captivity when Jerusalem was destroyed and her population deported to what is now Iraq in 587 BC:

> Comfort, comfort my people, says your God.
> Speak tenderly to Jerusalem,
>   and cry to her
> that her warfare is ended,
>   that her iniquity is pardoned,
> that she has received from the LORD's hand
>   double for all her sins. (Isaiah 40:1–2)

Isaiah looked both backward and forward, as was the custom of the prophets. Looking backward, he likened the coming exodus from Babylon to the old Exodus from Egypt. He spoke of making a highway in the desert, just as God had made a way through the desert the first time (see Isaiah 40:3).

Looking forward, Isaiah prophetically foreshadowed the final exodus God would accomplish when Christ would lead his people through death to life. That's why the evangelists read the prophecy as completely fulfilled not by the return of the Jews from captivity in Babylon but by the Messiah, as heralded by John the Baptist (see Mark 1:1–4). For the ultimate deliverance is not from geographic exile but from the exile from intimacy with God, who is our true home. It is the loss of life with God—and that deepest resultant mourning—that the gospel comes to comfort.

All true words of comfort do the same thing Isaiah does in that passage to some degree or other. We are called, however feebly, to look back on goodness and forward in hope. God builds on this pattern by reminding us of what he has done for his people and urges us to attend to the good that he will yet do. False comfort, in contrast, urges us to numb or distract ourselves with lies or booze or some other drug.

Not all mourning is private. A whole world can feel it, as we did, for instance, after the assassinations of the sixties and after September 11. But public or private, mourning can be immensely fruitful, spiritually speaking. The world abounds with examples.

September 11 is again instructive: The manifestations of courage, nobility, love, and prayer that issued from the wounds torn in the side of our nation show what riches we can discover in mourning. The blood that poured out of our hearts that day was an intimate sharing in the blood that poured from the wounded heart of Christ. Many knew both his anguish and his consolation. That is why the Ground Zero Cross remains, to this day, a potent source of consolation and healing for so many.

On the other hand, just as there can be false comfort, so there can be false fruits from mourning. It can be stillborn as bitterness, despair, rage, and vengefulness. Blasphemy as well as blessing can proceed from mourning.

The point of the beatitude is that a blessing comes to those who mourn due to the love of Christ, not the goodness of man. For God's tenderness is vastly greater than we can understand or imagine. The tears that Christ shed on the cross can put out the fires of hell for us, if we receive them. The suffering that we have to endure in Christ is not divine vengeance but a sharing in his own suffering. And even when chastisement comes to us for our real sins, it is ordered, always and forever, toward our final bliss and blessing, not toward our destruction.

But before, behind, and above all is that tenderness, a desire for our true comfort (not the TV or some alcohol-numbed counterfeit the world sells us), which is the deepest, sweetest comfort there is. It is a comfort that made Paul actually rejoice in his sufferings (see Colossians 1:24). It is a comfort so intensely beautiful that sane men have walked straight to their deaths rather than lose it. To taste it is to lose the desire for the cheap imitations the world routinely offers.

When your hour of mourning comes, as it surely will, may you know the comfort God gives in Christ and drink of it deeply.

CHAPTER THIRTEEN

Blessed Are the Meek

The third beatitude continues Jesus' tradition of transmuting lead into gold. Just as nobody wants to be poor and nobody wants to mourn, so nobody wants to be meek. That's because we think of the meek as doormats and dartboards. We assume the meek are timid little people who scatter like mice when somebody of consequence clears his throat. But our Lord does not say, "Blessed are the weenies." St. Joan of Arc was neither a weenie nor a wimp. Nor was St. Paul. Nor, of course, was Jesus.

That should be our first clue that to be meek is not to be a wimp. It is rather to be filled with the awesome power of the Holy Spirit and to not be defined by earthly power. It is to know who you are, where you are coming from, and where you are going, as Jesus did. It is to be at home in your own skin and not afflicted with the itching envy of somebody else. It is to be free *inside*. And to be free is to find that the whole world is yours already, freely given by the Lord of heaven and earth.

Jesus makes two remarks that bear on this sense of interior freedom and confidence that is the true mark of meekness. First he says, "Fear not, little flock, for it is your Father's good pleasure to give you the kingdom" (Luke 12:32). Second, he comments that men of violence tried to take the kingdom of heaven by force (see Luke 16:16). The paradox of this is that heaven is impregnable to such people, while it is wide open to his "little flock." Why? Because you cannot kick down a door that stands wide open.

It is the poor in spirit—the people who don't think they have the "right" to heaven, the simple, the humble, the gentle—who find, to their astonishment, that heaven has come looking for them, with an invitation engraved on the hands of the host who died to win it for them. While men of violence are off killing people and blowing up buildings to establish heaven on earth, heaven himself is quietly welcoming the wounded, the weak, the foolish, and the other victims that these *ubermenschen* have trampled in their pride. Indeed, the meekness of God is such that he prays even for such men when they crucify him and labors to transform them from violent persecutors and into saints, as he did Saul of Tarsus.

Those who are meek—who are so comfortable in their skin that they can lay down their pride and be the least—are not weak but almost inconceivably strong. When St. Maximilian Kolbe lay down his life for a fellow inmate at Auschwitz, it was not the Nazi executioners who were in charge. It was the victim. Kolbe played the Nazis like a fiddle, offering himself as a "useless priest" (according to their measure of malice) to rescue a man with a family and win for himself the crown of martyrdom.

Similarly, Paul says of Jesus:

> Though he was in the form of God, [he] did not count equality with God a thing to be grasped, but emptied himself, taking the form of a servant, being born in the likeness of men. And being found in human form he humbled himself and became obedient unto death, even death on a cross. Therefore God has highly exalted him and bestowed on him the name which is above every name, that at the name of Jesus every knee should bow, in heaven and on earth and under the earth, and every tongue confess that Jesus Christ is Lord, to the glory of God the Father. (Philippians 2:6–11)

In the worst act of injustice in the history of the world, it is the victim, not the victimizer, who is in charge, precisely because he knows his life is at the disposal of his Father. That is why Jesus says of his life,

"No one takes it from me, but I lay it down of my own accord. I have power to lay it down, and I have power to take it again; this charge I have received from my Father" (John 10:18).

We have, in the long run, the same power—by grace. For we too shall rise on the Last Day to everlasting glory in the risen Christ, to dwell forever in the new heaven and the new earth. That, by the way, is the full meaning of "the earth" that we are to inherit. In the old covenant the promise was about the inheritance of the Promised Land. But as the old covenant was provisional and ordered toward the dawn of the new and everlasting covenant, so the covenant blessings were also provisional—pointing forward to the fullness of blessing in the new covenant.

That is what Hebrews is getting at when it says of the ancient patriarchs:

> These all died in faith, not having received what was promised, but having seen it and greeted it from afar, and having acknowledged that they were strangers and exiles on the earth. For people who speak thus make it clear that they are seeking a homeland. If they had been thinking of that land from which they had gone out, they would have had opportunity to return. But as it is, they desire a better country, that is, a heavenly one. Therefore God is not ashamed to be called their God, for he has prepared for them a city. (Hebrews 11:13–16)

Some people have a hard time believing that the ancient patriarchs could have been hoping for the heavenly homeland. Such people feel sure that the horizon of the ancient mind ended with purely earthbound hopes, such as making a killing in Canaanite real estate. All those "immortal longings" of the Christian tradition, it is thought, came later, to more "highly evolved" spiritual types. But this is to indulge in chronological snobbery: the notion that we are five thousand years smarter and more spiritual than our ancestors.

In fact, "immortal longings" have always been part of the human condition. There is no reason to doubt that the patriarchs were afflicted with the same sense of loss, longing, and hope that we are—especially since no story out of antiquity better evokes it than the story of the fall of man, which originates with the people who sprang from the patriarchs.

Indeed, we find precisely this hope for something that is rooted in the earth and yet infinitely transcends the earth in the Levites, who celebrated and sang all the psalms that speak of God as their "inheritance." The funny thing about this inheritance is that it is given to those who rejoice not because they got a lot of real estate from the Almighty but because they didn't get any. For Levites owned no property. The Lord alone was their inheritance.

St. Thomas Aquinas desired that same inheritance. In a vision God asked him to name his reward. Thomas's answer was instant: "I will have thyself." This is miles away from what we think of as meekness but is in fact precisely what Jesus means by it.

The witness and hope of the blessed meek is this: Seek first the kingdom of God, and all the rest, including the new heaven and the new earth, will be given to you as well.

CHAPTER FOURTEEN

Blessed Are Those Who Hunger and Thirst for Righteousness

The goods of this world, though they remain good, can be deceptive to a member of our fallen race. In certain moods of rude good health and the flush of adolescent insolence, it is all too easy to speak as though we *can* live on bread alone and (as postmodern professors never tire of saying) as though "everything is about power." But when the buffets and battering of real life rip away the veneer of consumerist comfort in which we muffle ourselves, we seek love and hope, not power—if we are wise and listen to the better angels of our nature.

We discover again that things like meaning, truth, beauty, goodness, and love are for our souls what bread is for our stomachs. We sicken of the empty calories of what passes for wisdom in this world. We find indeed that it is more vital to our life to know *why* we are alive than to merely *extend* life. We discover that we are desperate to know that there is goodness in the world and that we can know it, live it, and give it to our grandchildren. We find, in short, that we hunger and thirst for righteousness.

Simply discovering that is to grow up in ways that countless philosophers and academics in the bastions of clever postmodernism called "American universities" have yet to discover. If you hunger and thirst for righteousness, you find that you stop being afraid of and intimidated by the wisdom of this world. You discover that you are not stupid for ceasing to fear it. You find, to your surprise, that you are a grownup and a human being.

Of course, when you make this break with what people tell you to think and begin trying to think with Christ and his Church, one of the results will be that you will receive (as a sort of badge of honor) the title of "self-righteous." But what does *self-righteous* actually mean? For most speakers of modern English, it means, "I don't like you, and the principle you express belief in makes me very uncomfortable and angry." Indeed, in postmodern culture, there is basically no difference between calling somebody "self-righteous" and calling him or her "righteous." The words are functionally synonymous, and they both mean "Pharisaic" or simply "full of pride."

Now, this is a major change from biblical thinking. For self-righteousness is 180 degrees opposite to the biblical notion of "righteousness," not a synonym for it. To be called "righteous" in Scripture is a *compliment*, not an insult. It means something much closer to what modern English speakers mean by "a great guy" or "the salt of the earth" or even "a genuine hero" than the crabbed teetotaler, icy snob, or self-regarding gasbag we think of when we hear the word *righteous* today. When Matthew calls Joseph a righteous man (see Matthew 1:19, *NRSV*), he means that as a very good thing indeed. He is not in any way implying that Joseph is a rule-bound, unfeeling, moral calculating unit unable to sympathize with human frailty in his zeal to maintain his status as "holier than thou."

So what's the difference between righteousness and self-righteousness? The word *self*. A person who upholds a moral system (especially a difficult one) is not automatically self-righteous. He is only self-righteous if he maintains that he has the power to uphold his moral system on his own steam, because he is All That.

The proof is in Scripture. There we have it that the apostles and evangelists upheld an extremely high moral standard, one that even the Pharisees could not keep (see Matthew 5:20). But they were not *self*-righteous in doing so, even when they carefully (and quite obnoxiously, to their Jewish audience) repeated the denunciations the Master had uttered against the Pharisees, as "blind guides" and "whitewashed tombs" (Matthew 23). Why were these annoying apostles not self-righteous? Because they emphatically insisted that their righteousness came from Christ, not from themselves. Indeed, they carefully recorded the fact that, apart from Christ, they could do nothing; that left to themselves, they betrayed and abandoned Christ in his most desperate hour; and that they were quite capable of doing that again if they rejected the saving grace he offered them (see John 15:5; 18:17, 25–27; Mark 14:50–52).

A Christian moralist who upholds some unpopular principle or denounces some popular evil is not automatically self-righteous for doing so, even if he is annoying and shrill. Indeed, no small part of his shrillness may be due to the fact that he fears his weakness. Calling such a one "self-righteous" is as silly as saying that an alcoholic who loudly and belligerently refuses the blandishments of his friends to go to the pub is self-righteous. In such a case the Christian moralist is basically saying (as C.S. Lewis remarked about his own writings on Christian morality), "'My heart'—I need no other's—'showeth me the wickedness of the ungodly.'"[33] The Christian's shrillness in such a case is a reflection of his acute awareness of his own weakness, not a boast of his superior and self-sufficient virtue.

I suspect that about 99 percent of the people in the world whom opponents in moral debates declare to be "self-righteous" in fact carry in their souls a deep dread (and often a bitter memory) of some moral lapse, which drives them to strongly emphasize the point of morality under discussion. Their emphasis may well be muddle-headed (as in the case of the prohibitionist or the person who identifies smoking, cards, dancing, or TV with sin). But unless you can demonstrate that a person is making a moral argument that really is predicated on congratulating oneself for being without the need of divine grace due to his or her intrinsic goodness, there's really no sense in calling such a person "self-righteous." Obnoxious, shrill, irritating, loveless, hostile, and rude, quite possibly—but not self-righteous.

Having distinguished self-righteousness (that's bad) from righteousness (that's good), there remains the question of how we get this righteousness for which Jesus wishes us to hunger and thirst. The Christian tradition has hashed over three basic answers to that question: two of them false and one of them apostolic.

The first false answer is that of Pelagius, who argued that we are sinners because we sin. His prescription more or less amounted to saying, "Stop it!" All we had to do was pull ourselves up by our bootstraps and imitate Jesus (who was only sent as a model, not as the source of righteousness and power to carry out God's will), and we could be perfectly righteous on our own steam. This happy theory was stomped into the dust by Augustine for the simple reason that it is contradicted by the experience of every single human being who has ever lived. Heck! Even the sinless and immaculate Blessed Virgin never claimed to be righteous on her own steam but on the contrary sings, "My soul magnifies the Lord, and my spirit rejoices in God my Savior" (Luke 1:46–47). Nor was Augustine doing anything other than maintaining the profound wisdom of St. Paul in pointing out that, in fact, we sin because we are sinners, fallen in Adam and unable to save ourselves apart from the grace of Christ (see Romans 5:12–21).

For Augustine, as for Paul, sin is first and foremost a kind of spiritual birth defect. It is not so much a thing as the lack of something: the divine life in the soul. When our first parents fell, they lost this divine life, so they could not pass it on to us. We are born with a hole in our souls where the life of God should be, and our lives inevitably reflect that gaping wound in our sinful and disordered deeds.

Many sectors of the Reformation, following bits of Augustine's thought but not the whole thing, offered us another false choice. They agreed with Augustine that Pelagius was wrong about making ourselves righteous by grit, determination, and hard work. But they concluded from this that righteousness was fundamentally impossible for us to incarnate. They adopted a theory of "imputed righteousness," in which, as the classic image put it, salvation proceeded by God's covering the dunghill of our everlastingly corrupt humanity with the snow of Christ's righteousness. We remain the rotten monsters we always have been and always will be, but God "sees Jesus, not us," and so eternally *pretends* that we are righteous, even though our souls remain filthy and evil forever.

The problem with this theory is, well, what crummy sort of salvation is *that*?

There's a reason for that intuition: The idea is totally unbiblical. In fact, it's anti-biblical. That's why Jesus rebukes the Pharisees in these words:

> Woe to you, scribes and Pharisees, hypocrites! for you cleanse the outside of the cup and of the plate, but inside they are full of extortion and rapacity. You blind Pharisee! first cleanse the inside of the cup and of the plate, that the outside also may be clean.
>
> Woe to you, scribes and Pharisees, hypocrites! for you are like whitewashed tombs, which outwardly appear beautiful, but within they are full of dead men's bones and all uncleanness. So you also outwardly appear righteous to men, but within you are full of hypocrisy and iniquity. (Matthew 23:25–28)

Contrary to the theory of some Reformers, Christ comes to transform us and to make us participants in the divine nature (see 2 Peter 1:4), not to leave us as mere dunghills covered with snow or (to use the biblical image) as whitewashed tombs. True, *part* of the salvation process involves "imputed righteousness." As C.S. Lewis points out, this is how we raise our children: We treat them as kinder, more generous, more polite, and less self-centered than they really are. We teach them to parrot "please" and "thank you" and to "go through the motions" of civilized adulthood. We respond to their parrot talk and unreal politeness as though it were real. But precisely the reason we do this is not to leave them as selfish children, but to help them become mature, generous adults. As in a fairy tale, the ugly face puts on the mask of beauty and, in the end, becomes beautiful in response to the love showered on it. Grace is out to transform us, not to abandon us to our sin.

The fundamental insight of the Catholic tradition is that, ultimately, righteousness is not an abstract concept. It is not a legal fiction. It is not a mere moral state. It is not an ideal. It is not a rule, law, or command. Righteousness is a Person named Jesus Christ. To hunger and thirst for righteousness is, in the end, to hunger and thirst for him and for transformation into the fullness of his image and likeness.

Jesus knew this. That's why he gives us the Eucharist—his Body, Blood, Soul, and Divinity—which he has multiplied into food for a billion or so people and which still satisfies. It is a foretaste of the full satisfaction of heaven, where we shall sit at the marriage supper of the Lamb, not as everlastingly selfish children whose unreconstructed swinishness God pretends not to see, but as creatures who have really been completely cleansed of sin and made free and full participants in the perfect and glorious charity of the Trinity.

CHAPTER 15

Blessed Are the Merciful

"Whereto serves mercy / But to confront the visage of offence?" asks Claudius in *Hamlet*.[34] It's a good question and one that most of us don't really think about these days. That's because, increasingly, we are a culture that only has "mercy" on people who "can't help it" or "don't know any better." The problem is, that's not *mercy*; it's *excusing*.

Now, it's a fine thing, in any conflict, to search first for reasons why somebody who appears to have acted in malice did not really do so. We should always do this as our first act of charity. But a curious thing has happened in our culture, something that impinges even on Christians who ought to know better. As we reject God more and more, we allow more and more space for excusing evil and less and less space for admitting sin. Result: We have arrived at an era in which everything must be excused and nothing may be forgiven.

We see this in the weird combination of sophistry and merciless-ness that is postmodernity. Straining credulity, we create enormous and preposterous excuses for all manner of moral derangement precisely *because* we believe there is no mercy for sin. But straining our excuses to the breaking point comes at a cost. For when somebody finally *does* cross the line into what is undeniably sin (Nazis, child molesters, racists, terrorists, tobacco lobbyists, or some other perpe-trators of culturally inexcusable evil), we leap from excuses to absolute condemnation. We rain down on the heads of these condemned all the contempt and vilification in the world—and live in fear of what judgment awaits *us* should we fail to find an excuse for our own sins.

Apart from the miraculous forgiveness of the gospel, what else should we expect? When we look sin in the eye—real sin in all its vicious, willful, sneering, lying malice—well, who wants to forgive *that*? Why, if you did that, that monster who did that horrible thing would get off scot-free (we imagine)!

Forgive that fool I work with, the one who has been gunning for my job and spreading ugly rumors about me at the office water cooler? Forgive that nasty old woman who beat me when I was a kid and laughed at my tears? Forgive that zit-faced moron who deliberately keyed my car when I confronted him about tormenting the neighbor's cat? Forgive Osama bin Laden? NO!

But Jesus does, in fact, demand exactly that mercy of us. In fact, both in this beatitude and in the Our Father, he predicates any hope of our receiving mercy on our willingness to extend it to others. Be merciful and you shall obtain mercy. Forgive and you shall be forgiven (see Luke 6:37).

Of course, those of us who have been raised in a Christian culture know we are *supposed* to forgive. Like St. Peter, we might even be rather proud of our magnanimity: "Lord, the rabbis say you should forgive somebody three times, but since I'm that sort of chap, I'm going to go out on a limb and up the ante. Suppose we raise that to seven times?" Jesus' famous reply is *way* more than we bargain for: not seven times but seven times seventy times (see Matthew 18:21–22). Forgive everybody. Always. Forever. For everything. Indeed, Jesus tells us, "When you stand to pray, forgive, if you have *anything against any one*; so that your Father also who is in heaven may forgive you your trespasses" (Mark 11:25, emphasis added).

Note the completely unconditional nature of that demand. We are to forgive *whether or not the person against whom we have a grievance has repented.* That's because we are to love our enemies. To be sure, God will be their final judge, and if they die impenitent, then they will face the divine music. But since we are not God, it's above our pay grade to make that call. Our business is to extend forgiveness—in a word, love—to our enemies, whether they will have it or not. And coupled with that is the equally stark warning: If we do not forgive, neither will Jesus' heavenly Father forgive us (see Matthew 6:15). Period.

That is extremely difficult. So difficult, in fact, that I have long believed the most scandalous part of the Church's entire moral teaching lies here and not with all the yah-yah in the media about the various pelvic issues that so obsess our culture of apostate Puritanism. Everybody, apart from grace, recoils in fear and anger when we are confronted with the reality of Christ's teaching about mercy. Presented in such stark terms, it ought to give us real pause and make us ask, as the disciples remarked of another unbelievably difficult saying, "Who then can be saved?" (Matthew 19:25).

Who indeed? But the answer of our Lord also obtains: "With men this is impossible, but with God all things are possible" (Matthew 19:26).

This points us to a curious contrast between Jesus' teaching on mercy in the Sermon on the Mount and the way in which the Church after Jesus speaks about mercy. Some take this contrast as evidence that the Church has departed from the primal message of Christ. But of course, the only reason we know about Jesus' "primal message" is because the Church has carefully preserved it. So I think a wiser approach is to assume the contrast is a harmony and not a contradiction and that the teaching of the Spirit through the Church is of a piece with the teaching of Christ, who gives us the Spirit. What is that harmonious contrast?

Very briefly it is this: Jesus sounds as if he's saying God's ability to forgive you is predicated on whether you forgive. With Paul the lesson is clearly that your ability to forgive is entirely predicated on the mercy of God. So, for instance, Paul tells us:

> Put on then, as God's chosen ones, holy and beloved, compassion, kindness, lowliness, meekness, and patience,

forbearing one another and, if one has a complaint against another, forgiving each other; as the Lord has forgiven you, so you also must forgive. (Colossians 3:12–13)

So what gives?

The more precise question is "Who gives?" And the answer is God, who pours out his undeserved, unearned mercy on us, brings us into a covenant relationship with him in baptism, and enables (and expects) us to live out his life in the world. In short, the forgiveness of sins is a miraculous sign of his power and presence. We can't do it without him.

Our ability to forgive requires our first receiving the grace of God. Like the woman who washed Jesus' feet, we find that it is the one who has been forgiven much who is capable of forgiving much (see Luke 7:36–47). We are guided, not by fear of what awaits us if we act like the unmerciful servant, but by genuine love for God and neighbor—because mercy is liberating.

The good news of the gospel is that we are *sinners*, not merely victims or passive patients. We are not people so helpless about our moral choices that everything we do is a mistake. The gospel tells us, shockingly, that some things are excusable and *everything* is forgivable (save the pig-headed, calling-white-black refusal of forgiveness that is the blasphemy of the Holy Spirit). That's lovely to hear in our own case and it is why the experience of baptism and confession can be so overwhelming and beautiful for an adult received into the Church after a long life of sin.

But God's mercy is uncompromising: Just as we have been forgiven and loved when we were enemies of God, so we must extend forgiveness and love our enemies. This is not because God works on some system that says, "Forgiveness is a freebie the first time, but after that you have to earn it." Rather it's because God's love is *always* freely given, but our unforgiveness enslaves, hardens, and blinds us. The fist clenched in unforgiveness cannot receive the mercy of God with an open hand.

God commands us to forgive (and warns us against unforgiveness) not because he is a martinet with arbitrary rules who is longing to slam us when we step out of line. No, he commands us to forgive because he has been laboring since the day we were born to open us to his mercy, and he will go on doing it till the day we die and beyond. His command of mercy—and the blessing he places on it—is a promise of an eternity of peace and love, if we will abide in it.

The gospel stands in stark contrast to the contempt that is the sure mark of the presence of Satan just as joy is the infallible sign of the presence of the Holy Spirit. The "cycle of violence" is, above all, a violence of the soul. It sees the sinner, not as the object of God's love and Christ's redemption but as someone—something—beyond the pale of love. Such contempt is entirely satanic; it forms no part of the revelation of Christ.

The fundamental lie at the heart of such contempt is the belief that, by rejecting the sinful Other, we somehow ensure our own salvation. Christ exposes this lie in the strongest possible terms and assures us that it is only by having mercy on our enemy—that is, only by willing his good and not his damnation—that we open ourselves to the same hope.

The promise is as stark as the warning is strong: If we give no mercy, we can expect none. If we choose to show mercy, we shall—absolutely shall—obtain mercy.

CHAPTER SIXTEEN
Blessed Are the Pure in Heart

The Old Testament is full of purity rules aimed at keeping the Israelites from ritual defilement. We tend to read these regulations through glasses that have one lens from the ancient Christian tradition and one from a modern, post-Enlightenment perspective. The ancient Christian tradition recognizes (rightly) that the regulations on ritual purity in the Old Testament are no longer binding on us since the coming of Christ but were signs pointing to our need of him. The modern, post-Enlightenment view concurs that the regulations are no longer binding. But instead of looking to Christ as the reason they are outmoded, that view simply dismisses them as the savage taboos of a bunch of primitives that have been overcome by the spirit of progress.

Post-Enlightenment thought basically assumes that the Old Testament purity laws were nothing but prescientific attempts to avoid disease. It's as though "How do I avoid trichinosis?" and "What's the best way to keep the cooties away?" were the main questions that dominated the minds of the Old Testament writers. Such thinking commonly passes from alleged "scientific explanations" of how these ritual taboos arose to a triumphant and confident conclusion that we are, of course, four thousand years smarter than the people who shackled themselves with such barbaric nonsense. Thanks to progress, we are told, we don't fall for such ignorant taboos anymore. We know how to cook pork thoroughly, what causes leprosy, and how to refrigerate shellfish to avoid ptomaine. Gleaming Scientific Progress™ has perfected what the barbarians of the Old Testament were only groping toward.

The problem is that this whole "march of progress" scenario is an ill-advised way to approach Old Testament taboos. For one thing, it carries with it the modern aroma of contempt for childhood (particularly the childhood of the human race), as well as the modern hubris that the recent is always better than the old, and the future is better than all. More than this, it purports to read minds in supposing that, despite all insistence to the contrary, the focus of the sacred writers was not Israel's relationship with God but a quest for refrigeration, shampoo, and germ theory.

In contrast, the faith tells us that grace is not ashamed to build on nature and that children are often extremely valuable guides to essential truths. For this reason I think we do well to note that the purity regulations come from the childhood of the world, and so we do well by beginning there, rather than by attempting to press the Old Testament into modern, scientific boxes.

This is particularly true since, despite our alleged sophistication, we are not far from such childhood ourselves. If you don't think so, tell me how eager you are to handle someone else's used Q-Tip, scratch somebody's scaly skin, or touch a corpse. Even in cases where your intellect tells you that the chances of contracting disease are low, you don't want to do it. Why? The Ick Factor, that's why. It's "unclean." Like a child, you'd just as soon not touch it.

Similarly, before we feel too superior about our coziness with pork and shellfish versus the dietary taboos of ancient Israel, let's ask ourselves how many insect larvae we've eaten lately. Been a while since you've had a yen for brains? Or raw blubber? Once again, the notion that some things are simply too gross to put in your mouth (despite the fact that they are perfectly good food sources for the human body) is a more universal experience than we may have guessed.

Now, the interesting thing is that the New Testament has absolutely no interest in what C.S. Lewis called "chronological snobbery":

the notion that everything that preceded us is dumb and that the sole purpose of what went before is to lead up to us, because we are automatically more awesome. Instead the New Testament takes the question of "clean and unclean" and says, "You are on to something, but you don't know what you are on to. That whole intuition of uncleanness and revulsion, of which revulsion to pork and leprosy is a good image, has a proper object, but it's not the object you think."

Spiritual Pollution

The point of the Old Testament purity laws was that God took this natural human impulse to say, "Ick"—to regard certain things as "defiling"—and as with many other natural things, raised it by grace to teach a spiritual lesson. The image of food too gross to eat and things too disgusting to touch is an apt image of sin, which sickens the soul as much as the thought of eating maggots sickens your stomach.

The beauty of these ugly images of uncleanness—of some sort of contagion that infects, rots, and ruins—is that they really do powerfully communicate the *social* nature of sin, something that is lost on many moderns. The common belief sounded in our culture is "Who cares what somebody does in private? It doesn't hurt anybody else!" But the reality is that spiritual pollution, like physical pollution, is everybody's problem.

The funny thing is that those who deny the reality that sin can pollute a culture have no problem seeing that hydrocarbons can pollute an atmosphere. Those who are often most acutely sensitive to the dangers of exposing a region to electromagnetic radiation have no problem exposing that same region to electromagnetic radiation known as the lyrics of the latest cop killer rap on the radio or a filthy TV show. Such people are oblivious to the fact that sin is a sort of "air pollution" too and that what we exhale in private is inevitably inhaled elsewhere.

Take Madonna. I've never bought a Madonna album, never attended one of her concerts, never seen any of her (reputedly terrible) films. But because I don't live in a cave, I know a lot about her. So do you, most likely. I know all about the various blasphemies, the various incarnations and transformations from Material Girl to Crucified Dance Diva. I can't get away from it. It seems to be in the very water we drink.

Our kids can't get away from it either. And there's a lot of stuff much more toxic than Madonna out there. In a classic column Peggy Noonan described the culture in which the Columbine killers—and we—live. Our media culture brims with:

> ...was found strangled and is believed to have been sexually molested...had her breast implants removed...took the stand to say the killer was smiling the day the show aired... said the procedure is, in fact, legal infanticide...is thought to be connected to earlier sexual activity among teens...court battle over who owns the frozen sperm...contains songs that call for dominating and even imprisoning women...died of lethal injection...had threatened to kill her children...said that he turned and said, "You better put some ice on that"... had asked Kevorkian for help in killing himself...protested the game, which they said has gone beyond violence to sadism...showed no remorse...which is about a wager over whether he could sleep with another student...which is about her attempts to balance three lovers and a watchful fiancé...

"This," says Noonan, "is the ocean in which our children swim. This is the sound of our culture. It comes from all parts of our culture and reaches all parts of our culture, and all the people in it, which is everybody." [35]

God chose to use the image of pollution—of some all-soiling, all-pervading contaminant, like an infectious agent, or cooties, or leprosy, or sewage-stained water—to portray what sin is and what it does. Sin is not something that happens in private. It is not something we can keep to ourselves. It inevitably gets out, like the Ebola virus, and wreaks havoc with the whole of human society.

The problem is, it's easy to confuse the image for the reality. That is why Jesus had to starkly instruct his followers that it was not food that defiled but sin.

> "Hear me, all of you, and understand: there is nothing outside a man which by going into him can defile him; but the things which come out of a man are what defile him.". . . And he said to them, "Then are you also without understanding? Do you not see that whatever goes into a man from outside cannot defile him, since it enters, not his heart but his stomach, and so passes on?" (Thus he declared all foods clean.) And he said, "What comes out of a man is what defiles a man. For from within, out of the heart of man, come evil thoughts, fornication, theft, murder, adultery, coveting, wickedness, deceit, licentiousness, envy, slander, pride, foolishness. All these evil things come from within, and they defile a man." (Mark 7:14–16, 18–23)

His point, of course, was that the ceremonial Law of Moses pointed to our need for true cleansing—from sin, not from biological goo. We like to flatter ourselves that we are no longer prey to such an elementary confusion. But of course we are. And in more ways than one.

For instance, not only are we still hung up on food taboos, but as noted above, many postmoderns are also fond of the thoroughly gnostic tendency to identify purity with sterility. To be "pure" is, in this view, to be uncontaminated, germ-free, barren, scrubbed, metallic. In the words of the postmodern prophet Yoda, "Luminous beings are we, not this crude matter."[36]

This mind-set tends to see "pure" spirituality as one unsoiled by contact with matter and, most especially, with biological matter, such as the human body with its wide variety of fluids and sticky viscous substances—mucus, feces, urine, blood, sperm, spit, and sweat. Such a mind-set finds the Incarnation incredible. How could a holy God ever take upon himself the "sack of dung" that is the human body, much less submit to the indignity of undergoing all that slimy gynecology, living a life punctuated by visits to the latrine, then being manhandled by a bunch of mono-browed goobers in armor, beaten until the flesh flew and the blood spattered, spiked naked to the scandal of the cross, and bled dry by a stab to the heart? Better, such folk think, to say that the Incarnation was an illusion, that the proposition "This is my body" must be a spiritual metaphor for something *disembodied* rather than a bare statement of fact.

Be Fruitful

Similarly, the postmodern attitude that "skepticism is the purity of the intellect"—that the only sure thing is doubt—is a sort of adolescent avoidance of embodiment, which also identifies purity with sterility. It fears allowing our thoughts to become incarnate in the birth of a belief, a conclusion, an act, or a commitment, just as video-gaming twenty-something man-boys who live in their mom's basement fear the commitment of marriage and fatherhood. Put into practice, pure skepticism leads to imbecility, not wisdom or understanding. It is why Paul warns of those "who will listen to anybody and can never arrive at a knowledge of the truth" (2 Timothy 3:7). It is against this perpetual contraception of the thought process that Chesterton argues when he says, "The object of opening the mind, as of opening the mouth, is to shut it again on something solid."[37]

In contrast, ancient Christians identified purity not with sterility but with *fruitfulness*. Taking their cues from the testimony both of the Old Testament and of Jesus and his apostles, they reckoned that the body was *good*, like the rest of creation, and that things like sex, marriage, and babies, far from being snares and temptations, were good and even sacramental. In their view the central way by which God communicated his pure and Holy Spirit to the world was not through abstractions, Platonic forms, ideas, and concepts, but through the Word made flesh and through such media as water, blood, bread, wine, oil, human hands, and human voices. Such a view sees our humanity—with all its attendant animal gooiness, messiness, fangs, claws, hair, snot, and dandruff—not as "impure" but as profoundly sacred.

Indeed, for Jesus the source of impurity has nothing whatever to do with the organic side of human existence. Oh, to be sure, we can do wicked things with our reproductive organs (in lust), just as we can do wicked things with our digestive organs (in gluttony) or our mouths and hands (in bearing false witness or acting in anger). But the source of these evils is not the body but the soul.

So the gnostic notion of spiritual purity attained by mere disembodiment is exactly wrong. In the words of C.S. Lewis, "There's nothing specially fine about simply being a spirit. The Devil is a spirit."[38] Likewise, there's not a thing wrong with being a hairy biped full of blood, bile, snot, and poop. Every great saint (not to mention the Son of God) has been exactly that. The body is a beautiful creation of God. Purity—and impurity—originates not in these attributes of the body, but in the heart and soul. Sin and virtue are only *expressed* in the body.

In the same way, when applied to the life of the mind, the Christian insight identifies purity with the *union* of mind and truth, not with a mind too fearful of commitment to have contact with any truth at all.

To be sure, the Christian intellect is called to "keep an open mind" until the facts are ascertained. But it also insists that facts can indeed be ascertained: that we can know things, not only about this world but about God.

This means that the exercise of reason, including scientific reasoning, ultimately depends on an act of faith. Indeed, the very possibility of any mental act going forward rests, ultimately, on an unprovable article of faith: the faith that (1) the world is intelligible and (2) our acts of intellect will actually correspond to the structure of the world. So in the natural sciences, as much as in theology, we believe that we may understand. And in believing we discover again that purity of intellect, like purity of body, results in fruitfulness, not sterility.

The Treasure

One of the principal effects of purity (and impurity) is that it determines not only *what* we see but the *way* we see it. Scripture tells us, "To the pure all things are pure, but to the corrupt and unbelieving nothing is pure; their very minds and consciences are corrupted" (Titus 1:15). This does not mean that the pure of heart are Pollyannas who wander through life blind to the evil in people around them and whistling happy tunes to their adorable forest friends as in Disney's *Snow White*. It means that, like Jesus, they have no fear of "contamination" by contact with evil, so long as they are acting in charity and not in dalliance with the temptation to cooperate with evil. They are even capable of seeing the good that still remains in lives corrupted by sin. In contrast, the impure cannot see even the good that is there, and their cynicism drives them to name even white as black.

What lies at the root of this conflict is the same thing that lay at the root of Christ's conflict with the Pharisees. Dominated by pride and therefore closed to grace, the enemies of Jesus had only one way of dealing with impurity, whether ritual or moral: quarantine.

Indeed, the very name *Pharisee* means "separated one." The only way they knew to preserve their "purity" was by remaining untouched by contact with the defiled people and sinners they saw around them.

But Jesus proposed a new way. You can see it in the signs he works in Matthew 8—9. This is no grab bag of miracle tales thrown together at random by the evangelist. A common thread connects them all. In each story Jesus encounters somebody who, under the law of Moses, would render him "impure." But in Matthew 5—7 Jesus has gone up on the mountain like a new Moses and offered us in the Sermon on the Mount a new law, the law of the Spirit, beginning with the Beatitudes.

Now Matthew is going to show us the power of that law and of the One who gives it. So Jesus is shown meeting a leper, a Gentile centurion, demoniacs, the vile and despised tax collector Matthew Levi, a bleeding woman, and a dead girl. What do they all have in common? *The fact that contact with them, according to the Pharisees, made one impure.*

But instead what happens? The leper is cleansed, the Gentile and the tax collector are converted, the demoniac is delivered, the bleeding woman is healed, and the dead girl is raised, while Jesus remains pure and undefiled. Jesus had power to mix and mingle with tax collectors and whores, and it was they, not he, who changed. Moreover, he offers *us* this power as well, by his Holy Spirit. It is the power to see differently—and to live differently:

> That we, being delivered from the hand of our enemies,
>   might serve him without fear,
> in holiness and righteousness before him all the days of our
>   life. (Luke 1:73–75)

Jesus gets at this need for a change in the heart—in the *way* we see as well as in *what* we see—when he tells us:

For where your treasure is, there will your heart be also.

The eye is the lamp of the body. So, if your eye is sound, your whole body will be full of light; but if your eye is not sound, your whole body will be full of darkness. If then the light in you is darkness, how great is the darkness! (Matthew 6:21–23)

We are born looking for something. We think that we are looking for Mommy and Daddy, or a mate, or food, or money, or sex, or drugs, or rock 'n' roll, or power, or fame, or comfort, or knowledge, or wisdom, or success, or the beauty of nature, or any one of a million other things. But the surest proof this is not true is given not by those who never find these things but by those who do. Many people who achieve their earthly goals find they are miserable and blame the thing they sought for their misery. These despair and often die by their own hand. Others foolishly decide that if money or sex or food does not satisfy them, then *more* money or sex or food will. They waste their lives in "vanity and a striving after wind" (Ecclesiastes 1:14).

Meanwhile, those who are wise realize that whatever is good in what they achieve fails to satisfy, not because it is bad or because it is theirs in insufficient quantity, but because it merely reminds them of what they really want. These set about looking for what they *really* want. And they find, in the end, that what they want is to see the face of God. When they finally discover this truth, they let nothing stand in their way.

The beatific vision is the pearl of great price (see Matthew 13:45–46). Those who purify themselves from all that stands in the way by the power of the Spirit, who love all earthly things in the fierce awareness that they are entirely secondary to the love of God, who sell their worldly goods to possess it—these shall see God and be satisfied.

CHAPTER SEVENTEEN

Blessed Are the Peacemakers

"It takes three to make a quarrel," said Chesterton. "There is needed a peacemaker. The full potentialities of human fury cannot be reached until a friend of both parties tactfully intervenes."[39]

Chesterton was being funny, of course, but he was wisely pointing to a truth as well. It is the truth that keeps so many from being peacemakers—the truth that peacemakers will always be accused of being weenies and wimps by mutually hostile parties. The peacemaker is blessed by God; he is often cursed by man.

All the beatitudes pronounce a blessing on things that unenlightened, natural common sense tells us are not blessed. Being poor when everybody wants to be rich, merciful when everybody is screaming for blood, mournful when everybody wants gladness—calling these things "blessed" is decidedly counterintuitive. And to be a peacemaker—to suggest that the goal is ultimately to will the eternal good of even Osama bin Laden or Adolf Hitler and to love even them—is counterintuitive too.

"Love your enemy" is, in a word, bad for team spirit and unit cohesion and morale in a time of war. So peacemakers tend to get derided as "soft on terror," or as "counter-Soviet elements," or as "disloyal to the glorious Japanese Empire," or as "allied with international Jewry," or as "un-American," or as whatever the jargon the dominant regime uses to say, "Peacemakers threaten our ability to gin up violence in the populace against our designated enemy."

Note, for example, Pope John Paul II's response to the call for war with Iraq in 2003. John Paul, being a peacemaker, said firmly, "No more war! Never again war!" He sent an envoy—Italian Cardinal Pio Laghi—with a letter to President Bush, who placed it on the table unopened and proceeded to inform the cardinal at some length that war was "God's will."

> Cardinal Laghi told Bush that three things would happen if the United States went to war, the source recalled. First, it would cause many deaths and injuries on both sides. Secondly, it would result in civil war. And, thirdly, the United States might know how to get into a war, but it would have great difficulty getting out of one.
>
> He told the president that with peace nothing is lost, but with war great turmoil would be created, especially in the Arab world.[40]

Over a hundred thousand dead later—including over fifty thousand civilians—and with a crippled economy, a trillion dollars of debt, the United States transforming itself into a national security state, and the Middle East further from the promised dream of peace and democracy than before our adventure in Iraq began, Pope John Paul II and Cardinal Laghi look more prescient every day.

As does then-Cardinal Ratzinger (now Pope Benedict XVI), who famously responded to an attempt to get his support for that war by saying, "[The] concept of a 'preventive war' does not appear in the *Catechism of the Catholic Church*."[41] Indeed, the difference between the mentality of a peacemaker and that of the culture of death is illustrated by the attempt to use these words to justify violence as the first rather than the last resort. For recent years have seen the proliferation of a popular meme floating around on the Internet, arguing that the *Catechism*'s silence on preventive war means such war is therefore morally legitimate!

This is a breathtaking perversion of the Church's moral tradition. There is, in fact, *no* room whatsoever for pre-emptive war in Catholic teaching. This can be plainly seen by the *Catechism*'s actual teaching on just war:

> The strict conditions for *legitimate defense by military force* require rigorous consideration. The gravity of such a decision makes it subject to rigorous conditions of moral legitimacy. At one and the same time:
>
> - the damage inflicted by the aggressor on the nation or community of nations must be lasting, grave, and certain;
> - all other means of putting an end to it must have been shown to be impractical or ineffective;
> - there must be serious prospects of success;
> - the use of arms must not produce evils and disorders graver than the evil to be eliminated. The power of modern means of destruction weighs very heavily in evaluating this condition.
>
> These are the traditional elements enumerated in what is called the "just war" doctrine.
>
> The evaluation of these conditions for moral legitimacy belongs to the prudential judgment of those who have responsibility for the common good. (*CCC*, 2309)

The point is this: Just war doctrine has been formulated by the Church, not to give us a trigger mechanism so that we can roll up our sleeves and commence slaughter with a song in our hearts, *but in order to make it as hard as possible to go to war*. The point of just war doctrine, in other words, is to set up a series of roadblocks to slow down and restrain the human appetite for mayhem, vengeance, murder, and destruction which sinfully yearns for an excuse to be unleashed. The doctrine is formulated in such a way that *all* the requirements, not just one or two, need to be fulfilled in order for a war to be considered just.

The Church Teaches Peace

The first requirement is that the war must be an act of *defense* against an actual aggressor, not a preventative act of aggression against somebody you fear might be an aggressor one of these days. Similarly, the second criterion is that war must be a last, not a first, resort. Therefore, pre-emptive war is necessarily unjust war—because war is not something you "get" to do. War is something you tragically are forced to do as a last resort.

Pre-emptive war, being neither a response to an actual act of aggression nor a last resort, is itself *an act of aggression*. It should be as morally desirable to Catholics as would be the thought of amputating your healthy leg because you fear that in five years you might step on a nail and get gangrene. No Catholic should be eager to cut corners on just war doctrine—because war means innocents will die, women will be made widows, and children will be made orphans. That is why Joaquin Navarro-Valls, speaking on behalf of Pope John Paul II at the outbreak of the Iraq War in 2003, said, "Those who decide that all peaceful means that international law makes available are exhausted, assume a grave responsibility before God, their conscience and history."[42]

In short, the argument that the silence of the *Catechism* on pre-emptive war speaks in *favor* of it is like the argument that the silence of the *Catechism* on the subject of ritual cannibalism means that the Church is in favor of that. The purpose of the *Catechism* is to tell us murder is wrong, not to play a game of "Simon Peter Says." The Church is not obliged to laboriously spell out a one-million page list of every conceivable form murder can take.

The concern of the Church is to teach peace, not to find loopholes for war. That is why, before she gets to talking about the last-ditch extremity of war, Holy Church says:

By recalling the commandment, "You shall not kill," our Lord asked for peace of heart and denounced murderous anger and hatred as immoral.

Anger is a desire for revenge. "To desire vengeance in order to do evil to someone who should be punished is illicit," but it is praiseworthy to impose restitution "to correct vices and maintain justice." If anger reaches the point of a deliberate desire to kill or seriously wound a neighbor, it is gravely against charity; it is a mortal sin. The Lord says, "Everyone who is angry with his brother shall be liable to judgment." (*CCC*, 2302, quoting St. Thomas Aquinas, *Summa Th* II–II, 158, 1 ad 3; Matthew 5:22)

Deliberate *hatred* is contrary to charity. Hatred of the neighbor is a sin when one deliberately wishes him evil. Hatred of the neighbor is a grave sin when one deliberately desires him grave harm. "But I say to you, Love your enemies and pray for those who persecute you, so that you may be sons of your Father who is in heaven." (*CCC*, 2303, quoting Matthew 5:44–45)

Respect for and development of human life require peace. Peace is not merely the absence of war, and it is not limited to maintaining a balance of powers between adversaries. Peace cannot be attained on earth without safeguarding the goods of persons, free communication among men, respect for the dignity of persons and peoples, and the assiduous practice of fraternity. Peace is "the tranquillity of order." Peace is the work of justice and the effect of charity. (*CCC*, 2304, quoting Augustine, *City of God*, 19, 13, 1: PL 41, 640; see Isaiah 32:17; see *Gaudium et Spes*, 78)

Earthly peace is the image and fruit of the peace of Christ, the messianic "Prince of Peace." By the blood of his Cross, "in his own person he killed the hostility," he reconciled men with God and made his Church the sacrament of the unity of the human race and of its union with God. "He is our peace." He has declared: "Blessed are the peacemakers." (*CCC*, 2305, citing Isaiah 9:5; Ephesians 2:16, *JB;* see Colossians 1:20–22; Ephesians 2:14; Matthew 5:9)

A Place for Pacifists

This frequently ignored and overlooked instruction precedes the material in the *Catechism* on just war, because war is, in the Church's understanding, not the "natural state of man" (as certain pagans insist) but a major manifestation of sin. And sin is, for Catholics, normal but not natural. It is Calvinism, not Catholic faith, that says sin and nature are identical. Catholic faith points out the truth that sin does not constitute nature but destroys it. Therefore a philosophy predicated on the assumption that sin is natural is contrary to both nature and grace—and to the Creator and the Redeemer.

So while the Church *allows* for war when all alternatives to peace have been exhausted, her natural sympathy is with peace as our natural state, since we are created to live in peace. That is why she has left open a large place at the table for people who genuinely believe that it is always wrong to take up arms. (Indeed, pacifism was the original default stance of the early Church, since Christians could see no point in killing for a pagan Caesar who was persecuting them—a question that may become a living issue again as the postmodern, post-Christian state hardens into enmity against the Church.)

In this openness to both just war and pacifism, the Church basically lives out the counsels of St. Paul in Romans 14, recognizing that some people believe it morally incumbent upon them before God *not* to fight, just as others believe it morally incumbent upon them *to* fight. Our task is to not pass judgment and assume too quickly that those who disagree with our preferred approach are either bellicose Mars worshipers or cowardly ninnies. Our tradition honors both the warrior saint Joan of Arc and the pacifist Servant of God Dorothy Day.

The only place the Church draws the line is when either a pacifist or a just warrior tries to insist that anybody who disagrees with him or her is "not really Catholic." And in a culture where the great majority of Catholics are supporters of just war, it is vital that this majority not speak with contempt for pacifists, since as Holy Church reminds us, they "bear witness to evangelical charity, provided they do so without harming the rights and obligations of other men and societies. They bear legitimate witness to the gravity of the physical and moral risks of recourse to violence, with all its destruction and death" (*CCC*, 2306).

This is nothing new. The psalmist lamented over three thousand years ago,

> I am for peace;
>> but when I speak,
>> they are for war! (Psalm 120:7)

The Prince of Peace suffered insult when he acted peaceably toward sinners, tax collectors, and occupying Roman troops (see Matthew 8:5–13; 9:10–13). He refused to rain down fire on the Samaritans and to ask his Father for angels to prevent his arrest (see Luke 9:51–55; Matthew 26:53). That's because he was the real Messiah, not the secular messiah that fallen human wisdom is always hoping for. He knew that peacemaking is always a sacrificial act.

That's worth repeating: Peacemaking, as much as fighting in a just war, is a *sacrificial* and therefore priestly act. We don't like that. We much prefer *realpolitik* where somebody else suffers and dies for a good cause. But our faith is blunt about the ultimate mystery of peacemaking: The Son of God surrendered to crucifixion in order to reconcile the members of warring race with God and with one another and to bring about the only true and lasting peace to be had. As St. Paul says:

> You who once were far off have been brought near in the blood of Christ. For he is our peace, who has made us both one, and has broken down the dividing wall of hostility, by abolishing in his flesh the law of commandments and ordinances, that he might create in himself one new man in place of the two, so making peace, and might reconcile us both to God in one body through the cross, thereby bringing the hostility to an end. (Ephesians 2:13–16)

To make peace, therefore, means a sacrifice, since all peace is rooted in the peace of Christ, and the peace of Christ was obtained "by his blood." Jesus was able to do this because he is the Son of God. When we make peace, whether between nations or between quarreling in-laws or between squabbling teens, we are therefore sharers in his sonship—beloved children of God the Father, with whom he is well pleased.

CHAPTER EIGHTEEN

Blessed Are Those Persecuted for Righteousness' Sake

When I was in fourth grade, a rerun of *The Twilight Zone* was interrupted by a news bulletin announcing that somebody named Martin Luther King, Jr. had been shot. I had not the foggiest idea who that might be, but I could tell from my mom's worried face that he must be somebody important.

The next day, at the beginning of school, Mr. Vaughn asked us how many people had heard that Dr. King had been killed the night before. More than half the kids in the class cheered. I still had no clue who the man was, but my Mom and Dad had raised me to think that it was wrong to cheer when somebody gets shot and killed. It left a bad taste in my mouth.

It was my first experience with martyrdom for righteousness' sake. And as with many an onlooker, my response was at the most basic level a simple perception of injustice. Looking at the circumstances of King's death, I concluded, "Surely this was an innocent man." As a fourth-grader, I had no grand theory of race relations in the United States, no knowledge of our tortured history, and not the slightest idea of who King was, what he stood for, who killed him, or why. I just knew that he was, by all accounts, a decent sort who was gunned down while taking the evening air on a motel balcony.

I mention this incident because it seems to me that this beatitude appeals to the human conscience at such primal roots. Jesus pronounces a blessing on those who are persecuted not for the gospel's sake but merely for righteousness' sake—for being decent sorts; for sticking up for the kid being bullied; for being not St. Lawrence or St. Maximilian Kolbe but any Jack or Jill outgunned by city hall, any fighter in a noble but lost cause, anybody who ever went down swinging for the right side—even if that right side was just your little brother, wrongly accused of raiding the cookie jar.

The point of the beatitude is that such people are still connected to heaven, even when they don't realize it. Such folk bear witness to ultimate things like truth, justice, and love, even when they are fighting for what many an onlooker may regard as light years from such "religious" stuff as the "kingdom of heaven." Jesus himself is taken by many onlookers not as a spiritual figure but as a decent bloke who got the short end of the stick. Long before all the details are worked out, the full biographical details learned, the background filled in, and the gigantic implications seen in full, there is, in the persecution of Christ, the simple, elemental awareness that a great wrong has been done, a recognition that "certainly this man was innocent!" (Luke 23:47).

It was the inescapable conclusion not just of the pagan Roman tasked with carrying out the crucifixion but of swelling numbers of converts in ancient Rome. They were driven to the conviction that, whatever else might be going on, the followers of Jesus were innocent and did not deserve the insane cruelties being meted out to them by the mob. Indeed, the stark contrast of the martyrs' noble courage and the bizarre hatred of their persecutors filled onlookers with shame, repentance, and faith, first in the goodness of their victims and then in the goodness of the Christ for whom they gave their lives.

We see this juxtaposition in a sort of chemical purity in some of the moments of the Passion. The sheer gratuitous cruelty of the crowning with thorns, for instance, has always struck me in the way it evokes both pity for Jesus and a sort of embarrassed disgust, not just with the thugs who conceive and execute such a satanic parody of human creativity and whimsy, but with our whole race.

I sometimes fancy that at the end of the world, there will be a vast tribunal composed of all the angels and archangels, as well as all the unfallen races that may dot the planets orbiting the stars of the night sky: the hrossa, ETs, Oyarsa, and sundry other creatures whom God, in his wisdom, may have made and quarantined from us by the immense distances of space. When we all meet up at the inauguration of the new heaven and the new earth, they will be excited to meet at last the inhabitants of the Silent Planet called Earth, the one it is rumored was favored by a visit from God himself long ago. The excitement will be palpable. Who, they will ask, are these blessed creatures of Earth, and what beautiful tale will they tell of the festal celebration they gave the Beautiful One when he descended to be among them?

"What did you do to welcome him?" they will ask in expectant wonder. And we, God help us, will have to tell them the whole appalling story, that in addition to running him through a kangaroo court, subjecting him to horsewhipping and jeers from a mob of boobs and morons, and the typical dull-meat-cleaver justice of a bureaucracy, we paused before spiking him naked to a cross—just for one exquisite moment—to focus our hatred into a sharp, crystal-line needle of special attentiveness: a sadistic little crown of thorns to press down on the head of a man already trembling with shock and blood loss. Imagine the burning shame of having to tell *that* story to perfect childlike innocence.

It's the special vindictiveness, the attention to detail, the diabolical perversion of playfulness, the pure malice of the thing that removes from our race forever the ability to say, "I just never realized. Had I but known. Just following orders...." We shall have to look the choirs of heaven in the eye and say, "We come of the species that does *that*— and does it to perfect innocence."

The crucifixion, in short, is itself the demonstration of why God had to make recourse to such a desperate sacrifice to save us. It shows us what our species is capable of—and the mercy of God that is even greater.

Of course, we try to muffle this awful reality by shrouding it in time. We assure ourselves that people did this because they were barbarians living a long time ago. Those of us with small imaginations genuinely believe that, unlike our ancestors, we would not hate, persecute, and kill saints. We imagine we are two thousand years smarter and better than the people who put Jesus to death, just as Jesus' hearers imagined that they would not have killed the prophets (see Matthew 23:29–30). We think ourselves wiser than the people who despised Paul, Perpetua, Felicity, and Joan of Arc.

The reality is that saying, "But this is the third millennium!" is exactly the same as saying, "But this is Tuesday, July 7!" It's nonsense, and it completely overlooks the fact that we have done it again and again and again and again to Christ's followers and to the weakest and most vulnerable among us, in spite of his identification with "the least of these" (Matthew 25:40, 45). We did it to the black man, we did it to the red man, we did it to the Jew, we do it in unimaginable numbers to unborn babies, and we'll do it to a saint in a heartbeat. That's because saints still come to us in very repulsive forms, challenging our deepest and most cherished loves—and bigotries. They are antidotes to the popular lies of the age. And as Chesterton noted, because they are antidotes, they are often mistaken for poison.[43]

Jesus endured just such hatred. He and his followers were assured by all the leading authorities that his lot was with the wicked and that anyone who followed him would share his fate among the "accursed" who hung from the tree of the cross (see Deuteronomy 21:23).

But God has an altogether different opinion—and he always has the last word. He called Jesus his beloved Son and gave him kingship, not only over heaven but over the whole universe as well. The promise of the beatitude is that anybody who attempts righteousness and sticks with it while the whole world calls him a fool, blasphemer, coward, nigger lover, fetus fetishist, homophobe, friend of faggots, peacenik, self-righteous snob—or any of the other names pride assigns to attempted virtue—shall share in God's kingdom. And the paradoxical sign of our share in that kingship will be our share in his sufferings and the hatred of the enemies we are called to love and forgive (see Luke 6:27).

In the end, even such hate cannot touch our union with Jesus. We are called and graced to pray for those who despitefully use us—as he did. That is true union with him, and it is toward union with him that all the beatitudes are ordered. That's why the beatitude of those persecuted for righteousness is inextricably linked to the beatitude of those persecuted for Christ.

CHAPTER NINETEEN

Blessed Are Those Persecuted for Christ

They are about the most counterintuitive words in the Bible:

> Blessed are you when men revile you and persecute you and
> utter all kinds of evil against you falsely on my account.
> Rejoice and be glad, for your reward is great in heaven,
> for so men persecuted the prophets who were before you.
> (Matthew 5:11–12)

Yeah. Sounds great. Where do I sign up to get me some of that reviling, persecuting, and slander?

As we saw in the last chapter, the beatitude before this one pronounces a blessing on those who are persecuted for righteousness' sake. Taken in isolation, it would be easy to read that beatitude as a sort of generic "Rah, rah for the underdog" sentiment. But coupled with *this* saying of Jesus, it takes on a very different sense.

For this beatitude is a refinement and a refocusing of the one preceding it. Indeed, while I have broken it out from the saying preceding it so as to focus on it more closely, the Church's catechetical tradition has always taken "blessed are those persecuted for righteousness' sake" and "blessed are those persecuted for Jesus' sake" as a package proposition. That's significant, because it means that those who are persecuted for righteousness' sake are, whether they realize it or not and whether they like it or not, persecuted for Christ. So a pro-life atheist like Nat Hentoff who endures brickbats and ultimately loss of his job at the hands of people committed to the murder of the unborn is, whether he knows it or not, suffering on Christ's account.

This does not mean that salvation is guaranteed everybody who endures persecution. One can be unfairly persecuted and still be a jerk, a fool, or a dastard. The murder of SA brownshirt Horst Wessel may have been political persecution, but that did not baptize Nazism or render Wessel a martyr for righteousness.

But still and all, the fact remains that those who *do* God's will are doing it whether they think they are or not. They may be in for a happy surprise as they find themselves among the sheep who say, "Lord, when did we see *you* hungry and feed *you*, or thirsty and give *you* drink? And when did we see *you* a stranger and welcome *you*, or naked and clothe *you*? And when did we see *you* sick or in prison and visit *you*?" We have it on pretty good authority that "the King will answer them, 'Truly, I say to you, as you did it to one of the least of these my brethren, you did it to me'" (Matthew 25:37–40, emphasis added).

If this is true of those who suffer for Christ without even realizing it, how much more true is it of the Christian martyr, who endures all sorts of abuse and even goes to his death in conscious awareness that he does so for Jesus Christ? That is the ultimate meaning of the promise that lies behind this rather frightening last beatitude of Jesus. For though we admire martyrs, we don't want to be one.

This is especially true of Christian martyrdom, since (1) the devil really tends to pull out the stops for Christian martyrs (just read the hair-raising stories of the fiendish cruelties devised against them), and (2) these days you don't even get the payoff of the admiration of the mob that some of the early Christian martyrs got. William Tecumseh Sherman once remarked that the lot of a soldier is to die in battle and have his name spelled wrong in the papers. The lot of the soldier for Christ in our current culture is to get beat up in the culture wars (and in some parts of the world, killed) and have it covered by headlines like "Sectarian strife in Iraq" and "Anti-abortion religious zealot hits reproductive rights demonstrator in fist with nose." The general media narrative implies that radical Muslims fly planes into buildings because of religion—and by "religion" the media mean Christians and especially Catholics, who are every bit as evil, if not more so, what with their orphanages, hospitals, care of the poor, and network of charitable institutions that span the globe and dwarf all other undertakings for relieving human misery, poverty, and hunger. Somehow or other, every time a Christian is beheaded in Egypt the conversation in the media inexorably turns to such current issues in Christian criminality as the Thirty Years' War. In short, a basic rule of thumb in the media is to respond to every act of persecution against Christians with a *tu quoque* ("You too!").

And with good reason. We all remember the huge anti-Semitic pogrom that accompanied the release of *The Passion of the Christ*? The massive death and injury toll of zero and the property damage estimated to run somewhere in the range of absolutely no dollars stunned a world still reeling from the riots, murders, burning, and looting perpetrated by Christians following the debut of *The Last Temptation of Christ*. And this was promptly followed by the fatwas and assassinations caused by the release of *The DaVinci Code*. Is there anything more terrifying than the spectacle of the Our Lady of Perpetual Help Parish Women's Quilting Guild holy warriors screaming for the blood of the infidel?

Meanwhile, news of Christian persecution in China, India, Egypt, and, for that matter, Britain is wrapped in a litany of self-contradictory complaints and accusations about how Christians have it coming. Outrages are perpetrated against Christians every day around the world. Around 150,000 of them are murdered for their faith every year,[44] and the general response of our manufacturers of culture to this massive injustice is to simply ignore them and focus on the phantasm of some imminent "theocracy" if a bishop or preacher remarks that abortion is bad or heterosexual marriage is good. If that fails, nut jobs like Timothy McVeigh and Eric Rudolph (terrorists who both openly repudiated Christianity) are held up as "fundamentalist Christians" and the standard moral equivalence noises are emitted.

In short, a disturbing amount of media coverage (or non-coverage) of Christians sends the loud and clear message that they are a fanatical menace and when they get killed for their faith, it's no big deal. They're just Christians, after all.

Having said that, here's the thing: It's easy as pie to note the injustice of an anti-Christian media culture that is always looking for (or manufacturing) reasons to despise Christians and downplay the abuse heaped on them. I, for one, have no trouble following the natural course here. But the beatitude does not urge us to take the natural course and Jesus does not, in fact, follow my lead and spend a lot of time complaining about the obvious injustice of the world toward the Church, just as he did not spend a lot of time whining about his own persecution, passion, and death. To be sure, he warns the Church to expect injustices. But he does not instruct the Church, "When they persecute you, file a class action suit." He does not say, "You will be hated by all men, and you must call talk radio shows complaining about this fact." He does not urge us, "When someone strikes you on the right cheek, let it burn with resentment at the unfairness of it all." His counsel, as usual, is counterintuitive. He tells us to do things like cowboy up and take it—"He who endures to the end will be saved" (Matthew 24:13). And even more astonishingly, he says we should *rejoice.*

That would seem incredible and impossibly Pollyanna-ish, except that we know for a fact that his followers down through the ages have actually pulled it off. From the apostles in Acts, rejoicing that they had been found worthy to suffer for the name (see Acts 5:41), to Paul writing from prison, "Rejoice in the Lord always; again I will say, Rejoice" (Philippians 4:4), to St. Thomas More greeting the news of his condemnation with gratitude to the king who was ordering his judicial murder, to the martyrs of the twentieth century, such as Edith Stein, who wrote her fellow sisters on the way to Auschwitz to tell them her prayer life was going wonderfully well, we see that we really can rejoice and be glad about suffering for Christ.

Paul could write such words to the Philippians—instead of "Why me?" or "This shows the need for the proletariat to rise up and smash the oppressor!" or "God must really hate me and I deserve it!" or "This proves I really am a saint since people hate me!"—because he could see beyond his circumstances. Instead of being amazed at the injustice of the world to him or (worse still) assuming that being a victim automatically made him a saint (something every narcissist in the world assumes), he kept his eyes on Jesus and let him do the justifying. He kept in his heart the fact that Jesus had said, "If they have called the master of the house Be-elzebul, how much more will they malign those of his household" (Matthew 10:25). He focused on Jesus, not on himself or on his persecutors.

So did Peter, who wrote to his flock during the Neronian persecution that would cost him his life:

> Beloved, do not be surprised at the fiery ordeal which comes upon you to prove you, as though something strange were happening to you. But rejoice in so far as you share Christ's sufferings, that you may also rejoice and be glad when his glory is revealed. If you are reproached for the name of Christ, you are blessed, because the spirit of glory and of God rests upon you. But let none of you suffer as a murderer, or a thief, or a wrongdoer, or a mischief-maker; yet if one suffers as a Christian, let him not be ashamed, but under that name let him glorify God. (1 Peter 4:12–16)

This awareness that persecution was not strange but normal, meant that neither Peter nor Paul were shocked or surprised by it. They had no comforting modern mental buffer in their heads assuring them that people used to persecute Jesus' followers long ago in the early Church, but that such things are no longer to be expected because we are Americans or live in the twenty-first century. They knew that Christ's words were addressed to the Church throughout history and everywhere in the world, not simply to "the early Church." And so, they recognized as they sat in their cells awaiting execution that their sufferings were simply another way of being conformed to Christ, who was himself part of the prison population on the night before his own execution. Paul could rejoice, realizing that "to live is Christ, and to die is gain" (Philippians 1:21). He and Peter (following Jesus) endured what they endured, not because they couldn't wait to get out of this lousy world but because they couldn't wait to see the world renewed.

Paul knew that joy, not grief, is the final word that will be spoken. And he knew that our task is to ready our souls to receive it. So he knew that "he who sows to the Spirit will from the Spirit reap eternal life" and urged the Church, "Let us not grow weary in well-doing, for in due season we shall reap, if we do not lose heart" (Galatians 6:9).

Many ideological jailers of our post-Christian culture, the God-haters and acolytes of the new atheism, really detest the notion of Christians bearing up under suffering (whether through persecution or just due to the slings and arrows of outrageous fortune) in the hope of a heavenly reward. They declare that there is no God and denounce him as evil for permitting suffering while simultaneously complaining that Christians are vile mercenaries whose hope of heaven is a cheap childish consolation. They rankle at the thought that the talking piece of meat who is bound for the grave has hope for life in the next world.

This is curious when you think about it. Good materialists should operate under the assumption that since this life is all there is, it doesn't matter what Christians think about the afterlife. As secularists constantly bang on about how we create our own meaning, you'd think they wouldn't mind if a Christian holding his little girl as she gasps out her last breaths after a car accident finds consolation in the thought that she is going to her heavenly Father. But the instinct of the new atheist is to crush all such hope, to extinguish it by any means, and to resent any possibility of its fulfillment. He cannot rest with anything less than the complete triumph of death and the void.

And so the Internet is awash with new atheists expressing a strange contempt for Jesus' resurrection on the grounds that his passion wasn't a *real* sacrifice if he didn't have the decency to stay dead. Others condemn heaven as "escapism" (a subject jailers are particularly concerned with). In all this we hear the note that C.S. Lewis describes in his classic work *The Great Divorce:* the curious lust of evil to *extend* hell.[45] Like Lewis' ghosts, the God-hater is not content saying that this world is a cacophony of meaninglessness, a raw struggle for survival in which we must create our own hope and meaning. For some reason he is enraged when (by his own lights) Christians do exactly that with their (by his lights) imaginary heaven. He rails at such hope and wishes to stamp it out.

All other methods for coping with the immense sorrows and pains of life—drugs, alcohol, money, power, illicit sex, fantasies, philosophies, myths—are acceptable. But when a Christian speaks of heaven as his way of enduring the hardness of this world, suddenly the atheist speaks of the need to face the fact that all ends in cold and silence, that all hope is an illusion. As though he knows.

It is this desire to extend hell that ultimately drives the contempt for heaven as a "reward" among God haters and other jailers in the employ of the spirit of the age. They mask this hell-extension agenda with a moralistic condemnation of heavenly rewards as "working for a bribe." But this is rubbish. A man who marries for money is dishonestly working for a bribe. A man who marries his Beloved because she is his Beloved is obtaining the reward proper to his love. Likewise, the Christian who endures persecution or suffering for Christ does so in order to obtain Christ, who is his heavenly reward. Other rewards (virtue, joy, eternal life, power, communion with the saints) shall attend that reward, just as other rewards (family, home, new friends) often attend the grace of marriage. And such things have their place so long as they do not supplant the greater and more perfect object of love. None of that is "mercenary." It is simply the fullness of human life.

So it is idle to complain that Christianity is "selfish" in seeking heaven. Christianity is not and never has been purely altruistic. It does not and never has sought the extinction of the self or the rejection of happiness. The command by Christ to lose one's life has never been an end in itself but has always had in view the goal of gaining one's life (see Luke 17:33). There has always been an element of reward in it, because it is all about seeking the desire of our hearts—God in a communion of love—not about living in the icy loneliness of stoic pride. Christ frankly tells us that our reward will indeed be heavenly (that is, ordered toward relationship with him and his body, the Church), not mercenary.

Therefore, in this world we shall have tribulation, since this world is at enmity with him. But this world is not the end of the story. The next will be ecstasy beyond the power of eye to see, ear to hear, or heart of man to conceive. As St. Paul tells us:

> I consider that the sufferings of this present time are not worth comparing with the glory that is to be revealed to us. For the creation waits with eager longing for the revealing of the sons of God; for the creation was subjected to futility, not of its own will but by the will of him who subjected it in hope; because the creation itself will be set free from

its bondage to decay and obtain the glorious liberty of the children of God. We know that the whole creation has been groaning in travail together until now; and not only the creation, but we ourselves, who have the first fruits of the Spirit, groan inwardly as we wait for adoption as sons, the redemption of our bodies. For in this hope we were saved. (Romans 8:18–24)

Bolt, Robert. *A Man for All Seasons.* New York: Vintage, 1990.

Capon, Robert Farrar. *The Supper of the Lamb: A Culinary Reflection.* Garden City, N.Y.: Doubleday, 1978.

Chesterton, G.K. *Collected Works, Volume XVI: Autobiography.* San Francisco: Ignatius, 1989.

————. *St. Thomas Aquinas: The Dumb Ox.* Seattle: CreateSpace, 2010.

————. *The Thing: Why I Am a Catholic.* New York: Dodd, Mead, 1951.

Lewis, C.S. *A Preface to Paradise Lost.* London: Oxford University Press, 1961.

————. *Letters to Malcolm: Chiefly on Prayer.* New York: Mariner, 1973.

————. *Perelandra.* New York: Scribner, 1996.

————. *The Great Divorce.* New York: HarperCollins, 2001.

————. *The Pilgrim's Regress.* Grand Rapids: Eerdmans, 1992.

————. *The Screwtape Letters.* New York: Macmillan, 1970.

MacDonald, George. *Donal Grant.* London: George Routledge and Sons, 1883.

Orwell, George. "Politics and the English Language." In George Orwell, *A Collection of Essays.* Orlando, Fla.: Houghton, Mifflin, Harcourt, 1981. This essay is also available online at http://www.k-1.com/Orwell/site/work/essays/language.html as of May 5, 2012.

Pope John Paul II. *Evangelium Vitae.* Available online at http://www.vatican.va/holy_father/john_paul_ii/encyclicals/documents/hf_jp-ii_enc_25031995_evangelium-vitae_en.html as of July 16, 2012.

————. "The Language of the Body: Actions and Duties Forming the Spirituality of Marriage," General Audience, July 4, 1984.

Twain, Mark. *Mark Twain's Notebook.* Albert Bigelow Paine, ed. London: Hesperides, 2006.

1. "Benedict's First Encyclical Shuns Strictures of Orthodoxy," Ian Fisher, *New York Times*, January 26, 2006. Available on line at http://www.nytimes.com/2006/01/26/international/europe/26pope .html?_r=1 as of July 8, 2012.

2. "But however little one thinks of the Jewish tradition, it is surely insulting to the people of Moses to imagine that they had come this far under the impression that murder, adultery, theft, and perjury were permissible." Christopher Hitchens, *God Is Not Great: How Religion Poisons Everything* (New York: Twelve, 2009), p. 99.

3. Richard Rorty, *Contingency, Irony, and Solidarity* (Cambridge, U.K.: Cambridge University Press, 1989) p. xv.

4. Available at http://www.the-ten-commandments.org/romancath-olic-tencommandments.html as of May 4, 2012. The "Bible Ten Commandments" are from the *King James Version*.

5. "Couple Stand by Forbidden Love," Tristana Moore, BBC News, March 7, 2007. Available online at http://news.bbc.co.uk/2/hi/europe/6424937.stm as of July 9, 2012.

6. Walter Isaacson, "In Search of the Real Bill Gates," *Time*, January 13, 1997.

7. Robert Farrar Capon, *The Supper of the Lamb: A Culinary Reflection* (Garden City, N.Y.: Doubleday, 1978), p. 85.

8. C.S. Lewis, *Letters to Malcolm: Chiefly on Prayer* (New York: Mariner, 1973), p. 93.

9. C.S. Lewis, *A Preface to Paradise Lost* (London: Oxford University Press, 1961), p. 99.

10. Glenn Greenwald, "Repulsive Progressive Hypocrisy," *Salon*, February 8, 2012. Available online at http://www.salon.com/2012/02/08/repulsive_progressive_hypocrisy/singleton/ as of July 18, 2012.

11. You read that right. The President has claimed (and exercised) the power to decree in secret the death of any person in the world, citizen or not, he sees fit to kill, without evidence, arrest, trial, judge, jury,

counsel, or conviction. For more information, see Glenn Greenwald, "Confirmed: Obama Authorizes Assassination of U.S. Citizen," *Salon*, April 7, 2010.

12. Jo Becker and Scott Shane, "Secret 'Kill List' Proves a Test of Obama's Principles and Will," *New York Times*, May 29, 2012.

13. Pope John Paul II, *Evangelium Vitae, 73.*

14. See, for instance, http://www.ncregister.com/daily-news/pope-benedict-end-the-death-penalty/.

15. Teresa Lewis plotted to kill her husband and stepson for insurance money in 2002. Many people condemned her 2010 execution on the grounds that she expressed sorrow for her crime and that her mental capacity fell below the Supreme Court's permissible threshold.

16. Comment in response to Danielle Bean, "What Does the Catechism Say about Teresa Lewis?," *National Catholic Register,* September 21, 2010. Available online at http://www.ncregister.com/blog/danielle-bean/what-does-the-catechism-say-about-teresa-lewis as of July 18, 2012.

17. George MacDonald, *Donal Grant* (London: George Routledge and Sons, 1883), p. 750.

18. Walter Isaacson interview with Woody Allen, "The Heart Wants What It Wants," concerning Allen's relationship with his adoptive daughter, *Time,* August 31, 1992.

19. Meghan Daum, "Ashley Madison's Secret Success: The dating service caters to those wanting to have an affair," *Los Angeles Times*, January 10, 2009. Available online at http://www.latimes.com/news/opinion/commentary/la-oe-daum10-2009jan10,0,7649415. as of May 5, 2012.

20. Pope John Paul II, "The Language of the Body: Actions and Duties Forming the Spirituality of Marriage," General Audience, July 4, 1984.

21. C.S. Lewis, *The Pilgrim's Regress* (Grand Rapids: Eerdmans, 1992), p. 207.

22. James Frey, *A Million Little Pieces* (New York: Doubleday, 2003).

Oprah Winfrey selected for her book club this supposed memoir of Frey's years as an alcoholic, drug addict, and criminal. The book sold 1.77 million copies in 2005. Many of the incidents Frey reports were then documented by the *Smoking Gun* website to be outright lies, distortions or wildly exaggerated (see http://www.thesmokinggun. com/documents/celebrity/million-little-lies). When confronted about this on the air by Winfrey, Frey actually had the chutzpah to say that the the same "demons" that had made him turn to alcohol and drugs had also driven him to fabricate crucial portions of his "memoir."

23. Rigoberta Menchú and Elisabeth Burgos-Debray, *I, Rigoberta Menchú: An Indian Woman in Guatemala* (London: Verso, 1984). This book brought Guatemalan indigenous rights activist Rigoberta Menchú to international prominence and led to her being awarded the Nobel Peace Prize in 1992. David Stoll challenged the truth of some of her account in his *Rigoberta Menchu and the Story of All Poor Guatemalans* (Westview, 2007).

24. See St. Augustine, *Confessions*, bk. 2, chap. 4.

25. St. Thomas Aquinas, *Summa Theologica* II–II, ques. 110, art. 3, reply to obj. 2.

26. St. Thomas Aquinas, *Summa Theologica* II–II, ques. 110, art. 3, obj. 4.

27. St. Thomas Aquinas, *Summa Theologica* II–II, ques. 110, art. 3, reply to obj. 4.

28. St. Thomas Aquinas, *Summa Theologica* II–II, ques. 110, art. 4.

29. George Orwell, "Politics and the English Language," May 1945. Available online at http://www.k-1.com/Orwell/site/work/essays /language.html as of May 5, 2012.

30. Robert Bolt, *A Man for All Seasons* (New York: Vintage, 1990), p. 132.

31. Notebook entry, January or February 1894, *Mark Twain's Notebook*, Albert Bigelow Paine, ed. (London: Hesperides, 2006), p. 240.

32. Virgil, *The Aeneid*, Book I, line 462.

33. C.S. Lewis, *The Screwtape Letters* (New York: Macmillan, 1970), preface, p. xiii.
34. Claudius, in William Shakespeare's, *Hamlet,* Act 3, Scene 3.
35. Peggy Noonan, "The Culture of Death." Available online at http://www.orthodoxytoday.org/articles2/NoonanCulture.php as of May 15, 2012.
36. Yoda, in George Lucas's *Star Wars: The Empire Strikes Back.* 1983.
37. G.K. Chesterton, *Collected Works, Volume XVI: Autobiography* (San Francisco: Ignatius, 1989) p. 212.
38. C.S. Lewis, *Perelandra* (New York: Scribner, 1996), p. 93.
39. G.K. Chesterton, *The Thing: Why I Am a Catholic.* Available online at http://wikilivres.info/wiki/The_Thing/2 as of May 15, 2012.
40. Gerard O'Connell, "When Bush Put John Paul II's Letter on the Side Table without Opening It," *Vatican Insider*, September 17, 2011. Available online at http://vaticaninsider.lastampa.it/en/homepage/world-news/detail/articolo/guerra-del-golfo-gulf-war-bush-giovanni-paolo-ii-john-paul-i-juan-pablo-ii-8130/ as of May 16, 2012.
41. "Cardinal Ratzinger Says Unilateral Attack on Iraq Not Justified" (Zenit.org, September 22, 2002). Available online at http://www.zenit.org/article-5398?l=english as of May 16, 2012.
42. "Vatican: U.S., Backers on Iraq Held Responsible before God," *Catholic New Times,* April 6, 2003. Available online at http://findarticles.com/p/articles/mi_m0MKY/is_6_27/ai_111012339/ as of May 16, 2012.
43. G.K. Chesterton, *St. Thomas Aquinas: The Dumb Ox* (Seattle: CreateSpace, 2010), p. 5.
44. John Allen, "Recognize Martyrs around the World by Canonizing One of Their Own," *National Catholic Reporter*, May 4, 2012. Available online at http://ncronline/blogs/all-things-catholic/recognize-martyrs-around-world-canonizing-one-their-own as of July 19, 2012.
45. See C.S. Lewis, *The Great Divorce* (New York: HarperCollins, 2001), p. 80.